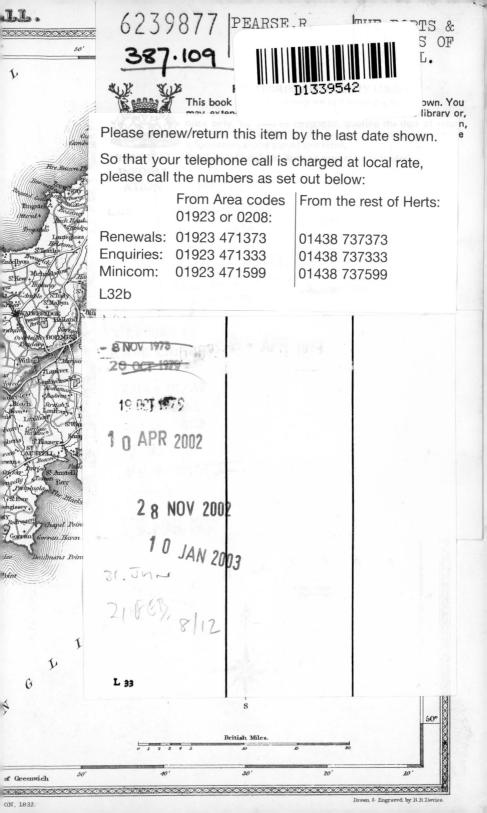
British Miles.

of Greenwich

ON, 1832.

Drawn & Engraved by B.R.Davies.

THE PORTS AND HARBOURS
OF CORNWALL

The
Ports and Harbours
of Cornwall

*An Introduction to the Study of Eight Hundred Years
of Maritime Affairs*

By RICHARD PEARSE

PUBLISHED AND PRINTED BY H. E. WARNE LTD.
EAST HILL, ST. AUSTELL, CORNWALL

CONTENTS

ILLUSTRATIONS

PREFACE

CORNWALL, with a rugged coastline more than two hundred and fifty miles long, stands at the entrance to what has been, for more than eight centuries, the world's busiest shipping lane. Projecting into the Atlantic between Wales and Ireland on the one flank, and Normandy, Brittany and the Bay of Biscay lands on the other, it found itself close to or virtually intersecting several medieval sea-trading routes.

The presence of alluvial tin in its soil, and of the fishing and fish-curing industries on its coasts, brought it a little trade in the second half of the twelfth century when the Crusades were having the effect of stimulating European commerce. Ships came into the safe Cornish estuaries both to trade and to seek shelter from storms, pirates and enemies. The county inevitably became a small centre of commercial and shipping activity.

When on the opening of hostilities between England and France in the year 1294 King Edward I began, in pursuance of state policy, to transform the south-western counties into a new and strong maritime region to supplement the East Anglia and the more vulnerable Cinque Ports groups of seaports, and thus increase the country's potential naval strength, Cornwall entered a new epoch, becoming a seafaring as well as a sea-trading county. Henceforward it was to build large numbers of ships and furnish the seamen to sail in them.

The irregular and hilly terrain throughout the county made communication difficult in every direction, and since almost the whole of its commerce was carried by sea the use of the shortest routes between the coast and places in the interior was of primary importance. The number of small ports and harbours increased as economic activity—tin mining, the fisheries and agriculture—grew and spread up and down the length of Cornwall. Very much later, in the new era of tin and copper mining and the much enlarged fisheries in the eighteenth and nineteenth centuries, the number of ports in regular use was extremely high, and almost every sheltered cove and beach at one time or another received or dispatched cargo-laden sailing vessels. Many a harbour served a district or hinterland no larger than three or four miles wide by about five or six miles deep.

This coming and going of ships, this seaborne commerce that has now been going on for eight hundred years without interruption, is but one aspect of Cornwall's rich maritime past. Other aspects, but not all of them, are touched upon in these essays. They include (a) incidents and proceedings that belong to the embryonic beginnings of the permanent Naval Executive, the Admiralty of England; (b) the administration of justice to the seafaring community in even the smallest harbours by courts of law sitting under the open sky and close to high water mark and using an internationally recognised code of customs and laws of the sea; (c) the international character of the early tin trade; (d) the flourishing business of well organised piracy in the fifteenth century; (e) the construction of artificial harbours on the open coast outside the estuaries; (f) the strongly democratic spirit in the governance of small borough ports; (g) the epic service of the lifeboats and, (h) the brief but brilliant epoch of the wooden merchant schooners in the nineteenth century.

This then is a brief summary of some of the things we may expect to find in Cornwall's long maritime life. We must not, however, exaggerate the county's part in our national maritime history, for it has not been important, except perhaps to a very limited degree in the fourteenth and fifteenth centuries. Yet we cannot overlook its fundamental significance, for Cornwall was the most typical and the most "maritime" of all our maritime counties, the one whose people were the most intimately associated with the sea, and whose known contribution to the nation's rich maritime life, if small, has been more varied than that of any other.

Indeed, a maritime history of Cornwall would be thoroughly representative of our whole national maritime story, for no other county is better qualified to present such a long and unbroken and, above all, varied maritime past. Yet this maritime history has never been compiled. As I am not a historian I cannot do it. I can only offer these brief essays as an introduction to the subject. They are neither detailed nor comprehensive, for they give only a rough outline of the origins, and a few of the activities of the ports, and have been compiled from only a selection of the abundant authentic historical material that is accessible.

My aim has been to follow a definite plan so that the whole work is brief yet presents a wide variety of the activities and aspects of the past whilst avoiding excessive repetition. There are therefore many obvious omissions from some of the essays, whilst several small fishing and trading places have not been mentioned. Their inclusion would have added nothing to our knowledge of Cornwall's maritime past. The Isles of Scilly, whilst hardly falling within the scope of my subject, have regrettably been excluded, since I have never been there and am therefore not qualified to write about them.

Some of the documents and works of reference mentioned in the bibliography are not directly concerned with the Cornish ports, either individually or as a group. Nevertheless they are, in my opinion, essential reading matter and an integral part of a comprehensive study of the subject, since they provide—especially those concerned with the pre-Tudor centuries—the broader European background to Cornwall's early commerce, and help to put into its right perspective the county's modest yet well established place in the maritime life and seaborne trade of medieval Europe.

It is against an essentially European background that the story of the Cornish ports must be considered; I have endeavoured to interpret this close relationship with Europe in these essays.

ACKNOWLEDGEMENTS

I cannot adequately thank all those who have generously given their help and advice in the preparation of these essays. To Dr. N. J. M. Kerling I am especially grateful for numerous helpful explanations accompanying her transcriptions of medieval documents made at the Public Record Office. I am also indebted to Dr. A. L. Rowse for a few recommendations made when the book was still only an idea.

Officials of the Public Record Office, the British Museum Reading Room, and of public reference libraries at Plymouth, Truro and St. Austell have been unfailingly patient and courteous in dealing with my enquiries for MSS. or works of reference.

My thanks are due to Mr. P. Howarth, Publicity Secretary of the Royal National Lifeboat Institution, for supplying statistical information and for allowing me to examine numerous volumes of *The Lifeboat* at the Institution's headquarters and make use of many reports they contain. I am grateful to Mr. Maurice H. Bizley for permission to make quotations from *Friendly Retreat*, his excellent history of St. Agnes; to the Editor of the *Western Morning News* for approval to adapt for these essays some material contained in articles published for me in that newspaper some years ago; and to Messrs. Percival Marshall & Co. Ltd. for consent to make extracts from and use material contained in Volume I of *Merchant Schooners*, by Basil Greenhill.

I am indebted to Mr. H. Dudley Snell, Clerk of Looe Urban District Council, for permission to reproduce the seals of the ancient boroughs of East and West Looe, and to Mr. Merville Matthews for the photograph of Porthleven harbour.

I have made copious use of a few of the well-known local histories written long ago by such authors as Jonathan Couch (Polperro), J. H. Matthews (St. Ives), Susan E. Gay (Falmouth) and A. E. Browne (Looe). Many of these local histories, if not impeccable works, are none the less valuable in that they not only contain authentic historical material, but also impart something of the picturesque daily life of the ports their authors knew so well, a rich and adventurous daily life that has disappeared for ever.

Mr. Percy G. Dalton of Falmouth made the drawings of the sailing vessels shown on pages 66, 97, 100, 105 and 120. The maps on pages 147, 148 and 149 were reproduced from originals kindly supplied by the Plymouth City Central Library, who also gave permission for the reproduction of the map on the endpapers and the plans of Fowey, Polkerris, West or Lower Polmear (Charlestown) and the Fal estuary shown on pages 44, 51, 56 and 71.

Finally, the invaluable professional advice and recommendations of Mr. Stuart E. Warne in matters concerning the production of this book are gratefully acknowledged.

R.P.

SALTASH

LIKE every other seaport borough that was founded in the feudal age Saltash owes its origin to industry and trade. The ancient tin mining industry, virtually a royal monopoly, which had been dormant since Roman times, was revived soon after the accession of Henry II, the first of our Angevin kings, in 1154. Dartmoor yielded tin, and on its western fringe Tavistock was appointed as one of Devon's four administrative centres and markets for the industry.

A seaport had to be found for the shipment of the refined metal. The chosen site, on the Cornish or right bank of the lower Tamar river at its narrowest point, a few miles below Tavistock but well concealed from the sea, was ideal. Enfranchised about the year 1190 Saltash, or Esse as it was then called, had its status as a seaport borough and market within the feudal framework officially confirmed.

Medieval merchants or their factors, who travelled in their ships, never went empty-handed; those who came to Esse to get tin would have brought merchandise to sell at its market, thus acquiring the liquid funds with which to buy the precious metal. The lord of Esse, vavasour of the honour or barony of Trematon, obtained for his borough the franchise to administer justice at the market and port by means of the appropriate legal machinery—a piepowder court and a maritime court.

Esse was one of the only two Cornish ports to make returns to the Winchester Assize of Customs, the first national customs system, which ran for twenty months from July 1203, and which levied a fifteenth subsidy on all foreign trade except on exports of tin. This commodity was exempt since it was already taxed under the stannary statutes of the year 1198 governing the re-organised administration of the industry. Since coastwise trade was also exempt from the subsidy the total extent of Esse's home and foreign trade cannot be estimated, but apart from shipments of tin it was undoubtedly small. The place must have looked forward to a promising future for it was still the only affranchised seaport between Dartmouth and Fowey, and it served an extensive region penetrated by the largest inland navigable water system in the south-west of England.

Yet Esse was to be eclipsed by the new port of Plymouth before the year 1260. The foreshore at Sutton Pool or Plymouth was an apanage of the honour of Trematon. Despite their common allegiance to the same feudal lord Plymouth and Saltash became rivals for the seaborne trade of the region. Events were to prove that the former was more favourably placed for expansion. Feudally, Saltash remained the mother port and had jurisdiction in all maritime matters over the whole of Plymouth Sound and the tidal waters of the Tamar and its tributaries. For national customs purposes only it came, after the new customs legislation of 1275, under the port of Plymouth.

Saltash, however, continued to grow slowly, and in the later Middle Ages it had its own ships and seamen venturing far afield and sharing in the steady national maritime expansion fostered by the Plantagenet kings. Many Saltash families were seafarers, the most prominent of them being the Slugges. We find them at the end of the fourteenth century carrying troops to Ireland for Richard II, and transporting pilgrims to Spain to visit the shrine of St. James the Martyr at Santiago de Compostela. In the early part of the fifteenth century the Slugges, with other merchants of Saltash, were engaged in the coastwise traffic to Southampton, taking tin and cured fish for transhipment in the big Italian carracks which called there twice a year. A vessel of John Slugge was amongst several from Saltash that were pressed into the service of conveying troops to Gascony towards the end of the long epoch of English rule in that part of France. And in 1442, when special measures were taken by the government to suppress piracy in the English Channel, two ships of Saltash, one of them belonging to John Slugge, were appointed for patrol work.

Perhaps Saltash should be remembered for the unusual exploit of the crew of one of its ships, the *Nicholas*, which, in 1438, traded to Finmark in defiance of the royal statute protecting the Bergen staple. Finmark, within the Arctic Circle, and Iceland, were then the most distant places reached by English ships, despite the ban on direct trading with those territories. Only a few ships a year had been venturing so far, for it was still a brave enterprise to take a small square-sailed vessel to the Arctic Circle, some 2,000 miles from the homely waters of the English Channel, unaided by charts or compass.

The Tudor seamen of Devon must have known all about their Plantagenet predecessors of only a hundred or so years earlier, whose seafaring experience and maritime traditions were at their disposal. The Slugges and many others—anonymous seamen of Saltash, Looe and Fowey—who endured the most difficult conditions in their small primitive ships, laid the deep foundations on which the Drakes, Hawkinses, Raleighs and Frobishers were able to build.

In 1584 Saltash obtained its Elizabethan charter of incorporation, granted ostensibly on the grounds that improvements to the quays and in the government of the port and town could be more easily achieved if the burgesses were created into a body corporate. With such small favours the government assured itself of the political support of many a Cornish borough and seaport. The grant had no other motive; improvements or not, everyone at Saltash must have known that their little port had no future and could never be a serious rival to Plymouth, just around the corner.

For centuries the mayors of Saltash held what was considered to be an admiral's jurisdiction within the whole port of Plymouth, and this privilege was symbolised in the reign of Charles II by the grant to the borough of the right to hold a model silver oar as one of its maces. By this time the mayor's authority in certain maritime matters was no more than an archaic survival of the jurisdiction of the medieval borough's maritime court. This much diminished authority was finally abolished in 1835 under the provisions of the Municipal Corporations Act. Despite this abolition Saltash continued to hold annually a so-called Water Court until 1885. This rather meaningless ceremony was a survey by boat of the water bounds of the borough's former jurisdiction, the Town Clerk reading the proclamation at every boundary point, calling on those who had any business with the court to draw near and give their suit and service. These pleasant perambulations occupied two enjoyable days.

For centuries until the coming of the railways the river Tamar and its main tributaries—the Lynher, which penetrated south-east Cornwall, and the Tavy—were commercial waterways carrying by both barge and sea-going ship some of the trade of the ancient towns of Tavistock, Launceston and Liskeard. In the late Middle Ages and in the Tudor period not only Saltash but also Landulph and Cargreen, two riverside villages immediately above it on the Cornish side, sent their own ships to sea, carrying cured fish and refined tin, mainly in the coastwise trade. In the great resurgence of mining in the nineteenth century some old and a few new quays on the banks of the rivers were very active. Those on the main river above Saltash served a region thick with metalliferous mines and granite quarries. Ships brought in coal, timber, machinery and other mining supplies, and took away refined tin, copper ore and granite. Much market garden produce from the more rural districts was sent, during the mining era, by barge and river steamer to Plymouth, whilst there was a heavy traffic in limestone from the quarries near Plymouth to countless riverside kilns all over the region.

All this water-borne trade, already reduced when the railways came to the region, continued until the first World War. Then the pattern of economic life changed completely. The old commercial waterways no longer see any trading ships or barges, and all the old quays are grass-grown and deserted.

LOOE

THE name derives from loch or lough—a lake or landlocked arm of the sea. A sheet of water resembling a small lake forms at high tide periods just above the town where the tiny East and West Looe rivers meet. These, in their joint course then divide the town into two parts before passing through the narrow neck of the harbour into the sea.

West Looe became a seignorial borough in 1243, and was one of the seaports for Liskeard, a tin mining centre. It also served a large and rich agricultural district, the prosperity of which was reflected in much church building and reconstruction during the long Bronescombe episcopate in the thirteenth century.

Looe shared in the maritime awakening of the south-west which began with the war against France in 1294 and continued for just over fifty years. Its seamen in growing numbers began to go through the rough harsh school of medieval seafaring, and by 1310 this tiny port had at least five ships of its own engaged in the Bordeaux wine-carrying trade.

The pressing needs of Edward I and Edward II for trooping, victualling and fighting ships for their expeditions against the Scots and the French transformed Looe into a minor supply port. At least thirteen times from 1297 to 1326 it was called upon to furnish its small quota of vessels, men, arms and victuals.

The methods employed for enrolling Looe ships for these campaigns were applied to most other ports in the kingdom, and throw much light on the rudimentary admiralty system of the period. We see how the central government maintained liaison with individual ports, and through which channels its instructions and directives were delivered. The financing of naval operations—payment of wages and victuals, hiring of ships and so on—is also adequately revealed.

The seals of the ancient and adjacent boroughs of West and

East Looe symbolise the medieval activities of the port. That of West Looe depicts an armed archer-mariner, whilst the East Looe seal shows a fighting ship equipped with protective shields and the newly introduced fore and aft castles for the use of archers.

The preparations for the invasion of France that was the opening of what became known as the Hundred Years' War brought about a remarkable development of this insignificant port. It was chosen as a centre of shipbuilding and of recruitment of mariners. In December 1336, on the eve of hostilities, the King's Council called an important conference at Westminster, to which were summoned the leading maritime experts from most of the ports in the realm, including Looe. These delegates, consulted for information about their ports, were then told what their communities were expected to furnish in men and ships should war break out. The conference came at the end of some forty years of badly organised naval administration; it was the first serious attempt by the government to assess and organise the whole of the country's maritime resources. It was in fact the most important step yet taken to forge an efficient admiralty system.

The outcome of the conference in so far as Looe was concerned was that in the following July the port placed at Edward III's disposal at least twelve ships manned by a total of two hundred and thirty-four seamen and fifteen "pages" or boys. Nine of the ships went to the Sandwich naval base in Kent to operate from there, and three others, each accompanied by a "constable"—a military officer—joined the fleet that was to carry to Antwerp and Dordrecht some of the wool requisitioned by the king to offer as a bribe for the support of the Flemings in his invasion of France by way of Flanders.

Then in 1342 Looe sent ten ships for Edward's vast expedition to Brittany, and simultaneously another five vessels for a campaign against Scotland. Again in 1346 and 1347 the port shared in the series of actions during the long siege of Calais, but the strength of the forces it supplied is not known. The famous Calais Roll, said to have been compiled some two hundred years after the events, credits the port with three hundred and twenty-five men serving in twenty ships. These figures might well be exact.

With a population in 1327, computed from the Subsidy Roll, of little more than two hundred souls, Looe could have provided the two hundred and forty-nine seamen for the expeditions of 1337 only by recruiting men from the neighbouring countryside, and from its group of international vagabonds, who seemed to gather in all medieval seaports. Relatively good wages, travel, excitement and adventure were attractions that easily enticed peasants away from the dreary monotony, squalor and sordid poverty of manorial life. The men also had the satisfaction of knowing that as enlisted seamen they were directly serving the king, and were paid by him.

An indenture signed at Looe in 1395, quoted in full in the Appendix section, was a typical form of contract drawn up between the Crown and the owner of a ship (who was also often its master) engaged for naval service. This selected contract was made between a serjeant-at-arms, acting for the king, and a Looe shipmaster, for a service to be fulfilled in Richard II's expedition to Ireland. As his reward the master of the *Katerine* was later granted a licence to carry in his own vessel from Looe sixty pilgrims going to Spain to make their devotions at the shrine of St. James the Apostle and Martyr at Santiago de Compostela. These pilgrim voyages were money spinners for shipowners and masters.

The three pestilences of 1349, 1361 and 1381 put an end to Looe's brief medieval glory. The port carried on its limited fishery, sending small consignments of cured fish to Southampton for the London market and for transhipment in the Genoese, Florentine and Venetian carracks that took on all their English cargo there. Looe also had a small part in the last expeditions to Bordeaux in the middle of the fifteenth century, and later also in the early Newfoundland fisheries. The greater importance of Fowey in the fourteenth century, and then the expansion of Plymouth, did nothing to help the growth of Looe, which lacked a capacious harbour and did not have any worthwhile trade.

Despite its insignificance Looe provides us with an excellent example of the governance of a democratic and publicly owned seaport. The Elizabethan charters of 1574 and 1588, granted to West Looe and East Looe respectively, mainly for political motives, made a clean break with the medieval past and laid down in concise terms the basic principles for the proper government of the twin boroughs and the port. Conferred by a despotic government, they were thoroughly democratic in character and spirit. There was none of the old Plantagenet brevity and vagueness about them. The boroughs were incorporated as legally constituted bodies and had their privileges, functions, powers, responsibilities and constitution clearly defined.

During the succeeding centuries the spirit of the charters was rigidly observed by the borough authorities and was apparent in many of their enactments and transactions. Following the national pattern the borough of East Looe, upon the granting of the charter, forthwith opened a Constitution Book wherein were recorded by-laws and ordinances that the new corporation were empowered to enact. These fixed the various tolls and dues payable by ships and merchants using the public quays, regulated such routine matters as the mooring or tying-up of ships, damage done by ships to the quays, walls and mooring posts, and compensation for such damage, the depositing of ships' ballast, and so on.

Now and again the corporation scrupulously took legal advice to ensure that in certain enactments it would not exceed the powers conferred upon it by its charters. A case involving a fundamental principle came up in 1788 over the by-law, imposing a duty on the importation and exportation of corn, that was confined to "strangers" and did not extend to townsmen. The corporation sought advice in these terms:

"That at that time and long after, no corn was imported or exported by the townsmen or inhabitants, but now for some years past, it hath become a great trade amongst them as cornfactors, to buy very large quantities of corn among the country farmers and to lodge the same in their lofts and cellars in the boro', and from thence to lade the same on board ships or vessels moored to or lying by or

near the publicke quays and places within the boro' for
exportation, and in like manner they sometimes import
corn without paying anything, in either case objecting that
they are not strangers as mentioned in the bye-laws. The
said quays at a great expence are repaired and kept in
repair by the Corporation. In the 29th Charles II the
quays, by a commission executed and returned into the
exchequer, were appointed as public exchequer quays for
lading and unlading goods, etc. charged with rates and
duties due to the King. The Corporation therefore con-
sider themselves liable to keep them in repair, but there is
no fund provided specially for that purpose. The bye-law
in question, you will observe, states no special ground on
which the duties are laid, or any particular purpose to
which the produce is applicable, and prescribes no ways or
means for charging or levying any of the imposed duties,
and sets no penalty or forfeiture on non payment, and no
distress or action at law is remembered to have been used
for enforcing the law. It has, however, been submitted to and
the duties paid, for such of the articles as have from time to
time been exported or imported. The Corporation are
desirous of making a new bye-law, for charging the townsmen and inhabitants with a duty of two-pence a ton on all
corn imported and exported by them, in case they have
power to do so, and to that end your opinion is desired."
The Corporation's legal adviser gave the following opinion:
"I think the Mayor and Free Burgesses by the Common
Council, have not authority under their Charter or otherwise to make a bye-law charging the townsmen and inhabitants of the boro' with a duty of 2d per ton for all corn
imported or exported by them. For the King can in no case
impose a new duty on the subject unless where it is for the
subject's benefit, which it does not appear to be in this
case, and the King cannot empower another to do what he
could not do himself."
The Corporation had thus to recognise that although they
had possession and even ownership of the quays they were not
vested with power to levy dues and tolls at will. Such a right

belonged only to the Crown, acting through the Exchequer. That this obscure municipal body could, in 1788, take such trouble over such an apparently small matter means that it knew the underlying democratic principle to be important. We have wandered far from this basic principle to-day, when dues, tolls and taxes are imposed with little regard for the individual.

Looe's trade had always been small, but it was varied. In the late seventeenth century the goods handled at the port included iron, tin, lead, hake, pilchards, conger, wine, soap, dowlas (coarse linen from Brittany), canvas (also from Brittany), pilchard oil (used for lighting lamps), corn and tobacco.

The port reached its lowest ebb during the Napoleonic period, a traveller there in 1808 finding it "despoiled of its trade by war", and exhibiting little else but poverty and discontent. The fishing and curing of pilchards were at a standstill, since the Napoleonic blockade had closed the Mediterranean, Looe's principal market, and there was a three years' stock on hand with no prospect of any of it being sold.

Once hostilities were over Looe, like so many other Cornish ports, marched forward to the expanding Victorian era. Increased commercial and agricultural activity caused a small canal to be cut to a point just below Liskeard. Opened in 1828, it had 24 locks in its brief six-miles course. Then the discovery up in the hills of copper ore and the re-opening of ancient lead mines, followed by the opening of granite quarries, brought much more shipping to the town's quays. A short railroad had to be laid down to bring from the hills north of Liskeard down to Looe the mineral ores and blocks of granite that strings of pack animals and waggons could no longer transport economically. In a distance of six miles the railroad climbed from 150 feet to 800 feet above sea level. The daily output of the mines and quarries was sent down the line in the evenings in detached trucks, each under the control of a brakesman. The empty trucks were hauled back the next day by horses.

Granite from the moorland quarries was supplied for forts or docks at Plymouth, Spithead, Portsmouth and in the Medway; for the new Westminster Bridge; for the Alderney, Dover and Portland breakwaters, and for other works. Much granite was dressed and polished before shipment; it included the base of the memorial supporting the monument of Prince Albert in Kensington Gardens, and dressed plain blocks for the Thames Embankment.

An observant traveller who was at Looe in 1851 has left a vivid description of what he saw of the port:

> ". . . curious old quays project over the water at different points; coast-trade vessels are being loaded and unloaded, built in one place and repaired in another, all within view . . . The inhabitants number some fourteen hundred; and are as good-humoured and unsophisticated a set of people as you will meet with anywhere. The Fisheries and the Coast Trade form their principal means of subsistence. The women take a very fair share of the hard work out of the men's hands. You constantly see them carrying coals from the vessels to the quay in curious hand-barrows: they laugh, scream, and run in each other's way incessantly. . . . As to the men, one absorbing interest seems to govern them all. The whole day long they are mending boats, cleaning boats, rowing boats, or, standing with their hands in their pockets, looking at boats. . . ."

Since the 1939–45 war the port has come back into occasional use, a motor coaster calling there once in a while to discharge a cargo of cement or coal. A few fishing boats are left there. The quays now serve as car-parks.

POLPERRO

OF several ancient frescoes discovered in 1848 during the restoration of Polperro's parish church at the neighbouring hamlet of Talland, perhaps the most interesting was that of a four-masted sailing ship. Two of the masts carried lateen sails, and flying from each masthead was a square green flag bearing a red saltire or cross of St. Andrew. The hull of the vessel was gaily painted with six bands in various colours, each band being overpainted with crosses of St. Andrew in a different colour from that of the band.

The fresco, evidently of late medieval date, was probably inspired by Mediterranean associations, since lateen sails and four-masted ships were not introduced into northern waters until Tudor times. It may have symbolised the maritime connections of the parish, or perhaps commemorated a participation in a crusade to the Holy Land.

Polperro occurs as Porthpira in 1303, and as Porpery in 1347. The modern name is an unfortunate corruption that crept in during Henry VIII's reign, for the little creek was a porth, but never a pool.

For centuries this old fishing harbour belonged to the lord of the manor, who erected the first stone pier there. Early in the nineteenth century the manor passed to one Zephaniah Job, a local banker and merchant of great integrity and honesty, who was employed by groups of local smugglers to look after their finances. He was receiving agent for the monies that had to be remitted to the merchants in the Channel Islands from whom the contrabandists obtained their goods.

The outer of the two stone piers was severely damaged by storms in 1774, in 1817—when thirty fishing vessels in the harbour were destroyed—and again in 1824. After this last disaster Ananiah Job, who had inherited the harbour rights from his uncle, did not possess the financial resources to repair the damage. He agreed to assign the quays to two squires of the parish, who, with the consent of the inhabitants, raised a repair fund by levying a new toll on coal discharged at the two quays. After a long period of discord and bickering the fishermen of Polperro, whose living depended on the security of the harbour in the south-easterly gales that frequently threatened it, consented to pay higher annual dues on their boats if the money were expended on a new pier to be erected on the left bank of the creek to give greater protection. Its construction took place after consultations had been held with the Tidal Harbour Commissioners at the Admiralty.

The government of small fishing ports, the proper application and collection of quay dues and tolls, and the state of repair of quays and jetties were, in the absence of a municipal corporation acting as the harbour authority, matters of some concern to the Admiralty. The Commissioners therefore recommended that the proprietors of the quays resign their rights to a board of trustees. Further improvements to the harbour were carried out in 1887, financed by public subscription.

Polperro had always lived by its fisheries, and carried most of its little trade by sea. Apart from coal, and salt for fish-curing nearly all its imports came from Plymouth, the merchandise being brought in a sailing vessel which maintained a regular weekly service between the two ports.

In 1850 Polperro had thirty fishing vessels giving direct employment to one hundred and forty-two people. Jonathan Couch, the Polperro antiquary, naturalist and historian, compiled some notes on the type of boat used by the fishermen in his day. Built locally, following the custom of all Cornish fishing villages, it was specially designed for use in this port that was situated in a narrow and dangerous creek.

> "They are of smaller size than those of Mevagissey and Mounts Bay, and adapted to the present conditions of the harbour; about 27 feet in the keel, and from nine to ten feet in the beam, and clinker-built. Remarkably stiff for their size, they are, when well handled, fast-sailing and safe. In ordinary times they carry but one mast, which has a sprit-mainsail and gaff top-sail; also a forestay

fastened to an iron beak on the stem, and carrying a fore-sail. They frequently hoist, besides, a mizzen, and rig out a bowsprit and jib. There is no deck, excepting the small cuddy between the first beam and the stem, and they are scantily furnished with a binnacle-box with its com-pass, and some rude contrivance for holding a fire. . . . In the time of hook-fishing the crew consists of two men; and the catch is divided into fifths, of which one is the share of the owner of the boat, and the remaining four are divided equally between the two men. . . . In the driving season the boat is manned by four men, and the proceeds are divided into eight parts, of which the boat and nets take half; the remainder is divided between the crew . . ."

In 1858 a new type of drift-net lugger was built at Polperro, from thirty to thirty-five feet in length and ten feet in the beam. Two other new types were subsequently built, being twenty-eight and twenty-three feet long respectively. In 1870 some twenty-five of these boats were owned at the port. The nets used for both seining and driving were made at Bridport, in Dorset, where rope cables for ships were being manufactured as far back as 1227.

Polperro was ideally placed for smuggling, and for some seventy-five years down to about 1825 it was much preoccupied with this activity. A. H. Norway described smuggling as one of the staple industries of Polperro:

"All joined in it; the smith left his forge, and the husband-man his plough; even women and children turned out to assist in the unlawful traffic. . . . Lusty seamen these, bearing no malice even when the revenue men scored a point. . . . It was a fine, breezy, lawless, defiant life, the natural continuation . . . of one much wilder and more lawless, of which the two, taken together, formed during long centuries of daily peril and seawarfare that type of hardy reckless sailor who won our battles in our time of need. . . . The pressgangs which swept along the Cornish coast in days of war knew that they were entering a huge storehouse of the finest fighting material that could be wished, an inexhaustible reserve of men whose daily trade was to encounter enemies either with force or guile, and whose ancestors for untold generations had been doing just the same. . . . For the point I insist upon is that there has never throughout our history been peace upon the western coasts until within the last three generations. If the seamen were not fighting with the enemies of England they were fighting with its law. . . . I say nothing of the morality of the life. I insist only that it was that which produced the thing we wanted when we went to war."

Jonathan Couch has left us a brief account of an adventure, typical of many, of a Polperro vessel. She was the lugger *Unity*, which had been commissioned and armed as a privateer during the Napoleonic wars. One morning at dawn off Ushant *Unity* found herself between two frigates flying the English colours, but Capt. Richard Rowett, her skipper, saw from their build and rig that they were probably French.

"All doubts were dispelled," writes Couch, "when a shot was fired across his bows to bring him to; and both immediately displayed the French flag. The nearest hailed him, and, considering the *Unity* to be their prize, ordered her to lie to whilst they boarded her. This order Capt. Rowett feigned to obey, and for the moment shortened sail; but when under the lee of the enemy, who were both lying to, quite contentedly lowering their boats, with their sails aback, he suddenly spread all sail, passing straight ahead of both frigates, took the helm himself, ordered the crew to lie flat on the deck. . . . The *Unity* soon escaped out of range without anyone being hurt. . . . Instead of being captured . . . this little lugger took many merchantmen as prizes . . ."

LOSTWITHIEL

IN the twelfth century Devon and Cornwall were the only sources of tin in the known world. This metal, in its refined form, began to appear as a regular article of trade at several foreign towns and seaports soon after Henry II came to the throne in 1154. We find the commerce in tin already established at Genoa and Messina in 1160, at Montpellier and Pisa in 1168, at Arles in 1170, and at San Sebastian and Bayonne also in 1170. A fixed rate of freight for the transportation of tin from the international market of Oléron to Bayonne was laid down in the statutes of the Society of Bayonne Ships, a corporate body set up between 1204 and 1214.

A regular "tin" route was established between Cornwall and the island of Oléron, whence the metal was sent forward through different ports: La Rochelle for Poitou and Anjou, Bayonne for the north of Spain and Navarre, and Bordeaux for Toulouse, Narbonne, Barcelona, Italy and the Levant. Another route for tin existed between Cornwall and London before the year 1200; from there the commodity was sent on to Bruges and the earlier of the Hanseatic cities.

So much for a brief outline of the early routes by which tin from Cornwall reached some of its destinations. We can now go back and determine from which port it was principally shipped. The de Wrotham Stannary statutes of the year 1198 make it abundantly clear that Bodmin was the centre of the industry in Cornwall, as well as the principal market for the sale of the refined metal. Already in the year 1180 the town was amerced for possessing an adulterine gild merchant, without which its trade could not be conducted, but the gild was not suppressed.

The tin mines themselves were shallow open excavations close to the streams that trickled through the moors of mid-Cornwall. The grain tin, eroded and washed away from the main lodes during the course of the ages by natural processes, was found on the hard "shelf" or rock beneath the alluvial deposits, anything from about five feet to twenty feet below the surface.

The nearest convenient point on navigable water to Bodmin —for the more important south coast, at least—was that where Lostwithiel now stands, and that was where Bodmin's seaport was built. The new township, whose parish church has not a trace of Norman work in it, became a seignorial borough at the latest in 1193. Its first charter of liberties embodied an ordinance whereby no stranger might keep a shop in the borough except aboard ship, implying that it was a seaport. This concession enabled seaborne merchants or their factors to sell to the townspeople the wares they brought in exchange for the tin and other commodities they wanted to buy.

In the returns to the Winchester Assize of Customs of 1203/ 1205 Lostwithiel occurs as the thirteenth port in the realm, out of a total of thirty-five, for the value of its foreign trade, excluding tin which, as we have already seen, was exempt from the subsidy. If we include this commodity, whose approximate value can be estimated from stannary records, Lostwithiel would occupy about the seventh or eighth place in the national list. Its foreign trade was greater in value than that of all the Cinque Ports put together, and gave it second place on the south coast to Southampton. In volume its trade was certainly much smaller, since tin had a very low bulk, but a very high value. In the returns Lostwithiel occurs as the port of Fawi, that is, the river or water of Fowey, for the town or borough of Fowey itself did not then exist.

Cornwall's trade with the south-west of France was the monopoly of merchants of Bayonne, and three of them—Petrus Chevalier, Augerus de Sancto Paulo and Wilhelmus Pere—were in 1202 granted the pre-emption of all hake and conger cured in Cornish ports. These fish they exported also to south-west France, although they came to Cornwall mainly for tin.

In 1198 two of these merchants purchased tin at the Bodmin market for an amount which, converted into our depreciated modern currency, would be equivalent to about £70,000, an enormous deal by medieval standards. Pere was still buying tin in 1213, when his ship and that of two other merchants were sequestered in a Cornish port for the purpose of carrying a group of knights with their horses and retinues to Poitou to join King John; directives were sent to the sheriff that the horses were to be accommodated amidships so that the merchants could stow their tin fore and aft.

During the Chancellorship of Ralph Neville from 1216 to 1222 the mayor and council of Bayonne laid a complaint before him, citing that one Fitz Nicholas, a Bodmin merchant, had failed to supply the balance of fourteen tons of a contract for tin which two Bayonne merchants had made with him at Bodmin in the presence of witnesses, and which tin had already been paid for.

These glimpses of the early tin trade point to Lostwithiel being the principal, although not the only, port of shipment. There were at this period only two other enfranchised port boroughs in Cornwall at which any foreign commerce was possible—Saltash and Truro. In the customs returns of 1205 the former is listed for an amount of duty which was only one-seventh of Lostwithiel's. Truro made no returns at all.

When he came of age in 1231 Richard Plantagenet, Earl of Cornwall, Henry III's younger brother, was granted the Cornish stannaries in fee. In due course this prince became one of the richest magnates of his epoch, deriving his wealth from wool and tin, and from the re-coining of the money of the realm. When, on his coronation at Aachen, he became titular head of the Holy Roman Empire, his income had to be in keeping with his exalted position; it is therefore not surprising that he carefully nursed the stannaries and steadily built up the export trade in tin. His relations with German merchants, who were of course his subjects, were particularly close.

In 1268 he acquired by purchase the borough of Lostwithiel and the nearby castle of Restormel. He granted the town a gild merchant and removed to it from Bodmin the administrative machinery of the Cornish stannaries. For reasons of prestige it was desirable that foreign merchants should buy their tin—a royal monopoly—at a royal borough adorned with all the trappings, paraphernalia and ritual in keeping with medieval princely dignity, rather than at a monastic town controlled by a prior.

If Richard did not live to carry out the full plans for Lostwithiel his son Edmund, who followed him as Earl in 1272, made a first-class job of it. He erected a vast and compact range of stone buildings which included the Hall of the Stanners (Coinage Hall) with tin storage cellars beneath it, the Hall of the Earldom Exchequer, the Shire Hall for county courts, the Stannary prison and other premises. Thus for the first time the stannaries had official buildings belonging to the Crown. The remnants of these ancient buildings, which give us some idea of their great original extent, have their various uses to-day.

Earl Edmund decreed that Lostwithiel should be the sole staple of tin in Cornwall, thus making it the leading tin market of medieval Europe. All the tin refined in the county thereafter had by law to be carried there for assaying, coining and weighing in preparation for the bi-annual sales. Edmund also centralised at Lostwithiel the civil, maritime and financial administration of Cornwall, transforming the county into what was virtually a palatinate. He was granted the rare privilege of appointing his own sheriff.

After Earl Edmund's death in 1300 Bodmin, Truro and Helston were also appointed as tin staples, but in 1314 the burgesses of Lostwithiel petitioned the King to have the sole staple restored on the grounds that these other towns had obtained their own tin markets only for the purpose of evading the coinage duty. And, the petition stated, if Bodmin were to remain a staple this would be to the disadvantage of merchants "venauntz de estranges teres", for the tin that was coined and sold at Bodmin had of necessity to be carried to Lostwithiel to be shipped from there to all countries, and this for the reason that it was the nearest and most convenient port. The petition had a favourable reception, one good reason given by the Council being that Lostwithiel "est villa regis".

Edward II had got heavily indebted towards his financiers of the Florentine Bardi Society, and in connection with his debts a Genoese merchant, Antonio Pisano, had in 1312 obtained a lien on the tin coinage dues, as well as authority to buy on the

king's behalf all the tin that might be coined in Cornwall. Two
years later the king made over to Pisano his right of pre-
emption. As it was much easier for Pisano to lay hands on all
the tin at one place than at several, the petition for the restoration of the sole staple, ostensibly compiled by the burgesses of
Lostwithiel, might very well have been instigated by him.

Pisano's abuses of privilege came to light in 1316 when the
tinners of Cornwall complained that after taking their tin to
Lostwithiel at their own expense they were paid only 42/-
per mwt for it, whereas Pisano was re-selling it at 72/-. So
uneconomic was his price that tin mining had been greatly
reduced, and the numbers of tinners fallen from about three
thousand to five hundred. With the resultant fall in exports the
people of Cornwall were no longer able to purchase in exchange
for tin the cloth, wine, iron, salt and other imported commodities they could formerly obtain. The tinners submitted a
petition to the king, and Pisano's privileges were withdrawn.

Upon the creation of the Duchy of Cornwall in 1337, supplanting the ancient Earldom, the king's first-born son, Prince
Edward, became its first duke. This prince's achievements on
the fields of battle earned him, after his death, the sobriquet
"Black Prince". His domains in Cheshire, Cornwall, Wales and
later in Gascony came under the direct control of his central
administrative system, replacing the simple household of his
infancy. Within this system Cornwall was once more a virtual
palatinate, with the local administration of its day-to-day
affairs entrusted to civil servants having their headquarters at
Lostwithiel.

The borough's maritime court, which had jurisdiction in all
matters appertaining to the law maritime, belonged to the
prince, and except in the unusual circumstances following the
Black Death plague of 1349 was farmed out to the mayor and
burgesses. As the court was not a court of record there exists
no account of any of its proceedings, and even references to it
are few. One such reference occurs in the year 1346, when the
Council of Prince Edward ordered the mayor of Lostwithiel to
make "speedy execution" of a judgement delivered in "the
prince's marine court". The court had awarded compensation

against the mayor and commonalty of Bristol in respect of a robbery committed at sea by Bristol pirates, the victims being three Lostwithiel merchants. These had complained to the Council that they had not received the compensation awarded by the court.

In February 1389 a ship of Brittany, chartered by John Sampson of Plymouth to carry some merchandise, sailed from that port to Lostwithiel. After the arrival of the ship the Lostwithiel maritime court sat to hear a complaint of debt by a merchant of Winkleigh in Devon against Sampson. Judgement was given against Sampson. John Curtys of Lostwithiel, seneschal of the court, seized part of the cargo belonging to Sampson in execution of the court's decision. But he also seized some of Sampson's goods in pursuance of an order from the Admiral of the South and West. Sampson then made a complaint of certain irregularities committed by Curtys. The outcome was an order to the Admiral's deputy to hear a plea by Sampson against Curtys regarding the theft of his property in the Breton ship. This plea was heard in an Admiralty Court which first sat at Lostwithiel at the first hour of the first tide on 28th March, 1391. The court sat again at the second hour of the following tide, and resumed its sittings on the next two days at Fowey.

This was the beginning of a long test case. Commissions were appointed to record statements made by witnesses for both the plaintiff and the defendant. These depositions were used in the admiralty court which resumed hearings at the Wool Quay in London. The case dragged on without, apparently, any definitive result for either party.

This case and another, which was heard by the Padstow maritime court and was followed by hearings in the King's Bench in London, led to the enactment of two new statutes. These were concerned with the franchise of the two admirals of the realm, about which there had been much ambiguity. The permanent office of admiral had been created in 1336 and the Court of Admiralty established about the year 1346, both for the main purpose of keeping order and dealing with piracy on the seas around England. But it was found that the admirals' courts were extending their legal business to matters other than piracy and encroaching more and more on the franchise of the maritime courts at the seaports. There were also suspicions that corruption by the admirals' deputies was hindering the normal course of justice.

The two statutes of 1391 and 1393, enacted following the Lostwithiel and Padstow cases, clearly defined the functions of the Court of Admiralty, by declaring that it had jurisdiction only in pleas arising from offences that took place on the high seas, and that it had no power to hear pleas arising from offences committed within the realm, that is, on arms of the sea— estuaries and tidal rivers—except in case of death aboard ship.

This clear distinction showed that the nature of maritime law was evolving; it tended to bring the traditional international code of maritime law, as practised in the local courts at the ports, closer to the common law of the realm, whilst retaining as international law only that part of it that could effectively deal with piracy on the high seas, where the victims were usually of a different nationality from that of the pirates.

With the countries of Europe already in the fourteenth century beginning to become nations and losing their character of private territories of kings, princes and feudal lords, piracy became more and more the subject of complaints made through diplomatic channels. It was becoming necessary to have it dealt with by a court of law having more effective power than the local maritime courts isolated in their small seaports. By the end of the fourteenth century there were signs that these local courts were becoming something of an anachronism; in the sixteenth century they disappeared as an effective means of administering maritime law.

But let us go back to the early fourteenth century, when maritime courts were still a normal aspect of port life. In Cornwall the mayors of the borough ports, of which the number had increased since 1203 when there were only three, were responsible for ministering justice to passing mariners and sea-borne merchants. In the unenfranchised ports the law was ministered by maritime courts appointed by and responsible to the havener of the Duchy of Cornwall, whose headquarters were at Lostwithiel. Cases, especially of piracy at sea, that were beyond the competence of the local courts at the ports, came within the jurisdiction of the Black Prince until he was appointed Governor of Aquitaine in 1363, and although he held an admiral's powers he had no admiral's court as such. Instead, such cases were dealt with by special commissions of enquiry set up by the Black Prince's Council and presided over by the sheriff. Commissions were appointed in 1346, 1347(2), 1351, 1355 and 1357(2), and there may have been still more.

Lostwithiel was Cornwall's busiest port until about the year 1355. For over one hundred and fifty years it had received ships from Vermeu and Castra in Spain; from Bayonne, Bordeaux, Oléron and La Rochelle; from Guérande and other ports in Brittany; from Rouen, Abbeville and Flemish ports; and from English ports. It exported cured fish, tin, butter, cheese, salted hogs and cloth. It imported a great variety of merchandise, amongst other things wine, fish-curing salt, iron, cloth, woad, garlic, corn, pitch and dried fruits. Although the customs accounts included Lostwithiel as part of the port of Fowey, they often indicated which cargoes were discharged at Lostwithiel itself.

The industry that had first created the port of Lostwithiel was now, in the middle of the fourteenth century, rapidly ruining it. Rubble, sand and soil from the tin streaming works, deposited by the tinners in the upper reaches of the Fowey river, were carried downstream until much of it met the tidal waters at Lostwithiel, where it silted up and choked the navigable channel. Strict measures were taken to try and remedy the evil, but the damage had got beyond the stage of repair.

The rival port of Fowey took away more and more of Lostwithiel's shipping, until by about 1400 the ancient borough had ceased to be a port for sea-going ships drawing more than about seven feet of water. Thereafter barges were used for the carriage of merchandise between the two places, this traffic continuing until about the end of the nineteenth century. Even then small ketches were able to discharge their cargoes of limestone at kilns on the banks of the river only a mile or so below Lostwithiel. Imported timber was sometimes discharged into the river at Fowey and then floated upstream to Lostwithiel on the incoming tide.

Until the setting up of the Fowey Harbour Board in 1870 the borough of Lostwithiel continued to collect keelage and anchorage from all ships using any part of the river for purposes of trade, as it had done for centuries. In the Tudor period it was also accounting to the Duchy of Cornwall Exchequer in the town for the profits of its maritime court. In 1535 the mayor answered for four courts held during the preceding twelve months.

Although an admiral was appointed for Cornwall[1] (as for other maritime counties) in the sixteenth century, he had no authority in the Fowey river in minor maritime matters, where by ancient custom the mayor of Lostwithiel was allowed to hold such jurisdiction. This archaic privilege of holding a maritime court was hardly more than a formality, a relic of Lostwithiel's golden age, but it was nicely symbolised, and its memory perpetuated, when King Charles II granted the borough the right to hold a miniature silver oar as one of its maces.

---

[1]   Subsequently two of them were appointed, one each for the north and south coasts, with authority to hear and adjudge pleas in Admiralty Courts which, under the reorganised Admiralty system, assumed some of the functions of the now defunct local maritime courts of pre-Tudor times. Lostwithiel and Saltash were privileged exceptions, retaining their jurisdiction.

FOWEY

THE early fishing hamlet of Fowey, taking its name from the river on which it stood, anciently Fawi, did not at first become a seaport because it was uncomfortably close to the sea and exposed to hostile attack. Nor for that matter was there any call for a trading place and seaport, since Lostwithiel, six miles up the river, was better placed for the neighbouring tin mining region.

But times could change, even in the Middle Ages. From about 1290 onwards England was to be in a chronic state of hostilities with France as well as with Scotland. Ships and seamen were badly needed. Hitherto most of them had come from the two main maritime regions of East Anglia and the Cinque Ports. The latter group of ports, situated in Kent and Sussex, came under frequent threats by the French, and were much too vulnerable to be safe. So a third maritime region—the south-west—was developed as a matter of state policy. It was not only less vulnerable to French attacks than the Cinque Ports, but it was also well placed for trade and communication with Gascony. And within it Fowey grew up and played a conspicuous part.

The use of Plymouth as an assembly and victualling port for large fleets of ships going down to Bordeaux in 1295, 1296 and 1297, and the presence there of King Edward I himself for a whole month in the spring of 1297, had an important impact on maritime affairs in Cornwall. The King scoured the ports, estuaries and creeks of the county for ships, men and victuals. New ports in the south-west were also required as bases for armed ships employed to hunt down French pirates and intercept French shipping proceeding around the Land's End to the aid of the Scots. The circumstances were such that the Fowey river, the heart of the expanding tin trade (for which Lostwithiel was still the port), was bound to benefit and see an increase in its general shipping activity. Very soon the "port of

Fowey", which always included Lostwithiel, was sending its own ships to sea, and it had not less than eight sailing from Bordeaux in wine-carrying convoys in the period 1303-1310.

From 1300 onwards Fowey was called upon to feed ships and men into the medieval navy; an odd vessel or two at first, almost every year, but sometimes more frequently, and then increasing until in 1337 it suddenly emerged as a major supply port. In that year it sent nineteen ships of its own, manned by five hundred and forty-seven fighting mariners, to operate with the fleet against French naval forces. This great achievement was surpassed in 1342, when twenty-nine Fowey ships with crews totalling over seven hundred and twenty men took part in operations against Scotland and off the coast of Brittany. The ships were employed mainly in victualling and in carrying troops and military stores, and fifteen of them embarked Welsh archers and spearmen at Plymouth for Brest.

How did Fowey, when it was probably less populous than it is to-day, with, at the most, no more than one thousand five hundred people of all ages living there, manage to muster at one time more than seven hundred and twenty men fit for service at sea? The figure is not legendary or suspect: the records giving the names of all the ships and of their captains, the number of men to each, as well as the pay rolls of the crews, are still in existence. The answer is that Fowey, like other ports at that epoch, attracted a host of vagabonds, outcasts, runaway feudal serfs and adventurers seeking freedom, excitement and money in travelling about from port to port and in fighting at sea. We can assume too that men were recruited at Lostwithiel, which had a population that in 1340 was a little larger than Fowey's, and from the neighbouring countryside.

What a place Fowey must then have been: its narrow alleys pungent with the stench of fish and refuse; packed with seamen and its own inhabitants dressed in richly coloured clothes; its taverns resounding with bawdy laughter and shouting, and re-echoing with talk and discussions in many languages—English, Cornish, Breton, French, Welsh and Irish—all of them medieval versions of these tongues. What a richness of life, humanity and spoken languages. How poor, by comparison, is modern Fowey.

The ships sent by the port to serve under the Crown were only its largest and most serviceable craft, and they were, for the most part, built in the river, and victualled and armed by the community. At that remote time, when civilised Europe was still extremely young and groping its uncertain way forward, the harbour, filled with sea-going ships, coastal and fishing vessels, barges and other river craft, was often more crowded than it is to-day.

Let us now jump ahead about a hundred years to Fowey's next great era, that of the pirates. Piracy had always been a normal characteristic of maritime life, a form of highway robbery at sea. All the maritime countries took part in it, and pretexts were easy to find in that age of more or less chronic warfare. Victims of piratical attack rarely obtained justice, since bribery and the slowness of communications made it difficult to hunt down the culprits. Commissions of enquiry were set up to deal with serious cases, but months or even years would pass before the malefactors could be found, and by that time they had committed many more piracies.

Robbery at sea had gradually evolved from spasmodic attacks on stray ships to a highly organised form of business financed by prosperous merchants. And because Fowey was both remote and happily situated at the entrance to the English Channel, then, as now, the busiest shipping lane in the world, it became the most flourishing centre of piracy in Europe. Its ships and seamen were feared by the merchants of all maritime countries and towns from the Baltic to Genoa.

It was soon after the year 1400 that the activities of four Fowey pirates, each working on his own account, drew attention to the port. The most successful was one Mark Mixtow, a licensed privateer whose small flotilla of three ships was supposed to be occupied in searching for and attacking enemy (French) vessels. But Mixtow could not resist the temptation to prey on just about every neutral ship he came across. He had perhaps some justification for harassing Flemish vessels, since the Flemings, whilst professing to be at peace with England, were, as vassals of the French king, sending out from Gravelines, Dunkirk, Nieuport, Biervliet and Ostende many armed pirate ships and privateers for the purpose of crippling English commerce. But it was after seizing a Hanseatic ship off Falmouth, looting the cargo at Fowey, and plundering the merchandise of several Spanish vessels that Mixtow became an embarrassment to the Crown and was asked to account for his deeds.

The family activities were carried on by another Mixtow, probably his son, who some years later brought off many successes, one of which was the capture of a Genoese carrack off the coast of Portugal. His men overpowered the Italian crew, took charge of the prize and brought her to Fowey, where her rich cargo was disposed of. An Italian carrack must have been a tremendous attraction, and people of every social condition—squires, government and Duchy officials, tinners and peasants—flocked into the town to buy at cheap prices the rich assortment of goods that otherwise rarely came their way. One haul made by John Mixtow was worth, calculated in terms of modern currency, something like £30,000.

It was not long before Mixtow was outshone by a newcomer, a Dutchman or German named Hankyn Seelander, who had been attracted to this notorious den of pirates that was a Mecca for fortune-seeking adventurers. In 1442 he and three other shipmasters were appointed by the government to patrol the Cornish coast with their own vessels in an attempt to suppress the evil. In the following year he drew attention to himself by committing three important piracies. He seized a ship of La Lègue in Brittany and distributed the cargo of wine, leather and iron amongst his accomplices at Fowey. Then he robbed the cargo of a Dartmouth ship, and soon afterwards pounced on a Spanish ship outward bound from Southampton with an enormous quantity of cloth.

An official government patrol vessel having set the example others soon followed. Things got out of hand, and nothing like it had been seen before. The next thirty years were Fowey's great heyday. Piracy became a highly developed form of trade, and everybody was in it—merchants who dealt in whole ship-loads of stolen goods, country squires and government officials who financed and armed the pirate ships and engaged the crews to sail in them, and the Customs men and port bailiffs under whose eyes looted property was sold to people who streamed in from a wide area.

A case of flagrant theft illustrates the lack of control by the government. In November 1449 two ships from the port went into Plymouth Sound and seized a big Spanish vessel that was sheltering from a storm. She was outward bound, fully loaded, for Barcelona and Valencia. Despite their safe-conducts the Spanish merchants were put ashore and their ship was brought into Fowey, where the rich cargo was put up for sale. The owners and victuallers of the two pirate vessels were a Cornish squire and three officials, one of them a lawyer, who held important stewardships under the Crown. Their names need no explaining: John Trevelyan, Thomas Tregarthen, Nicholas Carminow and Sir Hugh Courtenay, who held the big estate of Boconnoc near Lostwithiel. The men who presided over, or were members of, two subsequent commissions of enquiry into this piracy, were themselves either receivers of part of the loot or were operating other pirate ships. The Spanish merchants tried repeatedly to obtain redress through official channels in London, but in vain. Courtenay continued unhindered with his piracies, having at sea a vessel "manned with men of war well harnessed and arrayed", which brought ship after innocent ship into Fowey, where their cargoes were stolen and sold. Amongst the merchant pirates of Fowey were a Bodulgate, an Arundell and a Treffry, whose example only served as an encouragement to pirates of lesser stature.

In conclusion, one adventurous Fowey skipper, John Wilcock, deserves a mention. He was in command of the *Barbara*, a vessel owned by a large group of townspeople, which, between 15th May and 1st June, 1469, cruised off the coast of southern Brittany, and seized no fewer than fifteen ships.

Seen in its right perspective and against the distant background of the Wars of the Roses, all this fifteenth-century piracy was perhaps symptomatic of its period. It is to the credit of Fowey that it produced so many adventurous, if a little aggressive, seamen and merchants, who were strong and resourceful enough to put Fowey far ahead of all other ports in Europe in an occupation that, in its epoch, was not altogether unworthy, nor unprofitable.

The town of Fowey itself remained under monastic control until it acquired borough status late in the fifteenth century. It had therefore to wait unusually long to achieve this dignity, but it was an anomaly of the Middle Ages that a thriving seaport like Fowey could go without burgess liberties when personal influence could secure them for mere villages far removed from the coast and having scarcely any trade. Lostwithiel, the more ancient borough port, saw to it that the newer port should be kept without privileges. After 1337 the port of Fowey (as distinct from Lostwithiel) was let at farm for 40/- a year, well over £100 by present-day values. The amount of the rent indicates that a fair number of fishing boats was owned there.

In the late fourteenth century Fowey took over nearly the whole of Lostwithiel's seaborne trade, and was in turn superseded by Truro when in the fifteenth century mining activity moved westwards. Thereafter the port of Fowey languished, yet it was never completely without a little commerce. Shipping routes were maintained with Brittany, La Rochelle, Rouen, Flanders and several home and Irish ports. In 1450 a Fowey vessel, the *Cristofre*, traded to Iceland in defiance of the royal ban. Like the seamen of Saltash who had been to Finmark the skipper of the Fowey ship was fined, but pardoned a year later. The spirit of adventure was very much in evidence during that period when piracy was flourishing, but it was still something to be talked about when a ship went as far as Iceland.

Despite its decline Fowey still carried on its limited commerce in the Tudor and later periods without interruption. There was a regular import trade from St. Malo, Morlaix and Roscoff in goods such as soap, cloth, canvas and glass. Typical inward cargoes from other places were that of the ship *Ceader Tree* of Stockholm, bringing timber from Sweden; of the *St. Antonio de Padua* with a cargo of currants and "carrateells" from Argostal, a port on the Ionian island of Zephalonia, Greece; and mixed consignments such as one from San Lucar, of Spanish wine, raisins, olive oil, rice, soap, cork and cochineal. From Guernsey came brandy, wine and timber; from Jamaica sugar, and from Vianna Spanish salt, although this port, Viana do Castelo, is in Portugal.

There was also some variety in the port's exports. Regular shipments of tin went to Plymouth and Southampton; the ports of northern France took tin, wrought pewter and pilchards. One vessel in 1696 carried to Plymouth tin, barley and eight hundred bullocks' horns. The *Mayflower* of Fowey in 1697 went to Oporto with coal, tin, beeswax and pewter plates. Woollen cloth, nails, tin, pewter, pilchards and slate stone went to Guernsey; herrings to Madeira; and copper ore to Bristol. The middle of the eighteenth century saw an expansion in Fowey's pilchard trade, with frequent cargoes going to Venice, Naples, Leghorn and Bilbao. Polruan, the fishing village across the river that was farmed out in the fourteenth century for 20/- a year (more than £50 in modern currency), contributed a good proportion of the exported fish.

All these commodities and products represent a good portion of the great variety handled at Fowey, yet not a single one of these enters or leaves Fowey by sea to-day. Apart from china clay, and a very little imported coal, there is nothing.

The nineteenth century was relatively quiet, at least until the 1870s. Then came a great change. In 1869 an application was made to the Board of Trade for an Order for the construction of jetties and for the incorporation of a Harbour Board. Behind the application was the growing congestion in the little ports of St. Austell Bay, which could no longer handle expeditiously enough the fast growing output of the china clay industry. The Board of Trade had the wisdom to set aside the many objections to this plan for the development of Fowey. The construction of the jetties went ahead without delay.

From their inception these new jetties, linked by a new railway line with Par, and through it with numerous china clay mines both to the north-east and the north-west of St. Austell, handled about half the output of the industry. The jetties, discreetly concealed from the little town, now receive ships of up to 10,000 tons capacity, which take their cargoes to distant parts of the world. They go direct to Tasmania, India and North Africa; to the Great Lakes, and to the Atlantic seaboard of the U.S.A.; to Catania, Naples, Civitavecchia, Leghorn, Genoa and Barcelona; to many ports strung out on the continental coastline and to every corner of the Baltic.

With fewer loading berths than it had before the Second World War Fowey cannot increase its exports of china clay. It has in recent years lost some of its trade, since coasters of shallow draught prefer to load at Par, where the improved berthing facilities ensure good dispatch.

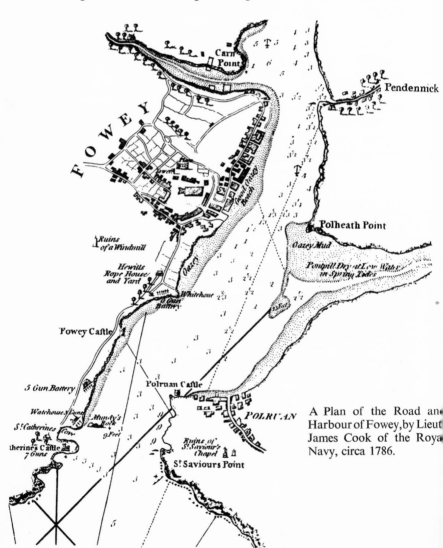

A Plan of the Road and Harbour of Fowey, by Lieut James Cook of the Royal Navy, circa 1786.

PAR

SEVERAL medieval seaports on our coasts have been left high and dry and have fallen into decay through the silting of rivers and estuaries. Par, a modern seaport and township, has been created by the same process. Waste rubble and soil from the old tin-streaming excavations in the moors a few miles to the north, together with normal river alluvium, brought down by a small fast-running river that was often a torrent in winter, filled up the estuary and pushed back the sea nearly two miles. Much of the township lies on a sandbank that was thus formed across the mouth of the old estuary.

It was on the seaward fringe of the old sandbank that ships were beached for the loading and discharging of their cargoes. Granite used in the construction of Rudyard's Eddystone Lighthouse, which was erected in the first half of the eighteenth century after the collapse of Winstanley's frail structure, was shipped from a now vanished loading point in the estuary. Stones were cut and then cramped together at the quarry up in the hills and, by means of what the local peasantry called "ploughs"—teams of several oxen and horses harnessed to waggons—were hauled through the rough lanes and the swampy flats to the ships. Granite from the same source used in Smeaton's Eddystone Lighthouse was also loaded into vessels at Par. As there was no loading equipment there Smeaton had to send ships that had their own tackle capable of lifting blocks of granite weighing $1\frac{1}{2}$ tons.

The Rev. Richard Warner, who journeyed through Cornwall in August, 1808, and described his experiences in a book published the following year, wrote that the sandbank, although above water at ebb tide, was awash at high tide, when travellers and their horses, in order to cross the estuary, either had to use the ferry or make a detour of some two miles up the valley to pass over the bridge at St. Blazey. It was not long before the estuary completely disappeared, whilst the sea has receded another quarter of a mile since 1808.

A few years after Warner's visit a large copper mine was

opened above the cliffs on the west side of the estuary mouth, whilst smaller ones began working within two or three miles. Ships in growing numbers came to Par with supplies for these mines, their cargoes being discharged on a beach close to the largest mine. The vessels were then loaded up with copper ore for South Wales.

The grounding and refloating of sailing ships were not easy operations on this coast where reefs and isolated rocks were concealed by the high tide, and when the wind whipped up a heavy inshore surf there was real danger of a wreckage. Obviously something better than a beach was necessary. The project for an artificial harbour at Charlestown, two miles to the westward, of which the construction was begun in 1791, stimulated interest in a similar one for Par. Plans were drawn up and submitted to John Smeaton, the eminent engineer, who approved them, adding one or two recommendations of his own. If the project was eventually abandoned we can only assume that the Anglo-French war and general trade depression had deterred the promoters.

By 1828 the pressure of mining, shipping and commercial activities demanded that the artificial harbour be constructed at last. Already more than two thousand people were working in the mines in the vicinity, and the number was increasing. The district had to be better served, whatever the cost.

The construction of the harbour was undertaken by Joseph Thomas Austin, a mining adventurer, banker and shipowner. The plan was, for its day, very ambitious. The area recovered from the sea, quite apart from the harbour's acreage of water, was—and still remains—greater than that of any other artificial harbour in Cornwall. Its extent can be judged by what it accommodates to-day: two large very modern china clay drying plants; large storage tanks and installations that receive the liquid clay by pipe-line; storage space for several thousand tons of dried china clay; an extensive but compact group of buildings containing mineral grinding plant; a dumping or storage ground for cargoes of imported felspar; a railway waggon repair shop; a coal dump and coal loading yard; extensive railway sidings; several buildings containing business offices;

three weighbridges; a gasometer with a coal yard; covered parking grounds for lorry trailers; and some two dozen private dwellings, several of them with gardens. Whilst most artificial harbours provide accommodation only for ships, and facilities for loading and discharging them, Par is unusual in that the built-up harbour area recovered from the open sea is also an active industrial centre.

The nature of its industrial activity has completely changed in the past thirty or forty years. Austin, whose father had married into the Treffry family of Fowey, and who himself assumed that name by royal licence in 1836, introduced a variety of industries, and his policy was continued by his successors. The industrial installations included a large smelting works for the desilverising of galena lead and producing pure silver; a brick works and kiln; a pilchard fishery; a shipbuilding yard; a sail loft; an important granite cutting and dressing yard, and a factory to make candles for the mines.

The designer of the harbour ignored the earlier plan of 1792 for an inner dock with lock gates. The port is therefore tidal, the ships sitting on the mud at low tide. Despite this big disadvantage an artificial harbour was infinitely better than a beach for handling loaded sailing vessels.

A typical product of the industrial revolution, Treffry was a man of imagination and inexhaustible energy. In our modern machine age companies or corporations with plenty of capital at their disposal would hesitate before the prospect of carrying out the task that Treffry took in his stride.

Treffry also erected an aqueduct-viaduct to carry a diverted stream and a small railroad across a deep valley three miles inland from Par. Six hundred and fifty feet long, ninety-eight feet high and containing some 200,000 cubic feet of granite, it still stands as a monument to its creator, although it has long since ceased to carry the railroad. The laying down of this line from Par made possible the opening of new china clay works, for it solved the problem of transporting the clay to the ships; the terrain was too difficult for horse-drawn waggons.

Since it was opened Par has been continuously busy. China clay, china stone, granite and copper ore were exported.

Treffry supplied his granite for such constructional works as the old Waterloo Bridge; London Bridge; the Thames Embankment; docks in the Thames and the Clyde; the Plymouth, Chatham and Gibraltar Dockyards; and the monument on the battlefield of Waterloo. Large quantities went to Gibraltar and Scotland, and one master of a Par schooner ran his vessel in the Clyde granite trade for twenty-five years.

The imports were mainly confined to the types of commodities and wares brought into all the Cornish ports serving the metalliferous mines. There were plunger poles and other types of timber from Scandinavia; hemp, barrel staves, iron, coal, mining equipment, tallow, pilchard-curing salt, canvas for making sails and all types of hardware and groceries.

The creation of the harbour consolidated and enlarged a strong local shipowning and ship managing community, which also had the closest interest in the local mines and other industries. Shipbuilders, shipbrokers, solicitors, mining adventurers, farmers, insurance agents, doctors and general merchants provided the capital that enabled the small closely-knit community to create, operate and control from within itself every side of its mining, industrial and shipping activities. The pumps and engines to work the local mines were manufactured by the community, which also built the sailing ships to carry away the mining produce, as well as financing and managing them. This kind of economic life is no longer possible; it belongs to a vanished age.

The locally owned wooden sailing ships often went into the deep sea trade in many parts of the western hemisphere. They wandered far, to Turkey and North America, to the remote corners of the Baltic and to the ports of Brazil and Argentina. They transported Italian marble, Newfoundland dried fish, South American hides, Mediterranean fruits, grain, iron ore, oil cake, timber, coal and other types of cargo.

The schooners that were built at Par and Fowey, and indeed elsewhere on the Cornish coast, were amongst the best of their kind. As the interests of the local industries—particularly that of china clay—extended from home and near continental to deep sea waters so the design of the schooners was evolved to suit the changed conditions. Instead of only four or five days the ships had to remain at sea for as many weeks; instead of popping into port when a bad storm blew up they had to stand up to the heavy weather of the North Atlantic and ride out the severest gales hundreds of miles from home, or perhaps hold on for two or three weeks in the doldrums waiting for a breeze. Capt. William Kellow, who died at Par in 1944 at the age of eighty-four, recounted how, when he was a boy, he used to swim around his father's schooner while she lay motionless for days under full canvas near the Equator. The changing lines of these schooners, their draught and beam, sail plan and cargo space were worked out and adapted from hard-won experience.

The men who designed and built these little merchant schooners in the tiny shipyards and in the creeks and coves around the coast had probably never heard of technical schools and engineering degrees. And some of them could hardly read or write. Yet their ships were not only seaworthy and efficient, but also graceful and attractive in appearance. They were beautiful creations compared with the ugly long-funnelled steamers that were beginning to compete with them, although not very successfully. In the end it was only the combination of large steamships and chains of bunkering stations that drove the small sailing vessels from the seas. The small steamers that replaced them in the trade of the Cornish ports were in turn quickly driven out by the modern diesel motor coaster.

To-day these clean and trim little ships, ranging in cargo capacity from two hundred to nearly one thousand tons, come to Par in steadily growing numbers. For the limited number of its loading berths this little port is to-day the busiest in the United Kingdom, handling the cargoes of more than 1,300 coasters a year. They take the produce of the china clay mines to ports all round the British Isles, and direct to Salonika, Algiers, Kenitra (in Morocco), Porto Marghera (Venice), Naples, Genoa, Barcelona, Bilbao, Pasajes, La Pallice, and to numerous ports strung out along the coastline of northern Europe to the far Gulf of Bothnia, as well as to many river ports, including that of the Paris Chamber of Commerce at Gennevilliers, on the northern outskirts of the city.

POLKERRIS

THIS hamlet, on the north-eastern shore of St. Austell Bay, one mile from Par, had a flourishing pilchard fishery until about the end of the nineteenth century. Above the beach are the ruins of the old Elizabethan "palace" or pilchard curing cellar, one of the largest ever to have been erected on our coasts.

The lord of the manor built a small pier somewhere about the year 1735 to provide shelter for the fishing boats owned there. Its construction was a purely benevolent work, since the negligible trade of Polkerris could never have made it a profitable investment.

A lifeboat station was opened in 1859. Two early rescues in 1862 and 1865 were unusual in that the brilliant seamanship of the lifeboatmen, who were local fishermen, saved not only the crews who were in distress but also their ships.

In 1865 the crew carried out two rescues in one day. Two ships driven helplessly before the gale were soon lying broadside on close to Par Sands with huge seas "running high over the top mastheads". In the dangerous waters the lifeboat lost six of her oars. The coxswain, to get the boat out of her predicament, let her drift, and then at the right moment hoisted canvas and skilfully steered her into Par Harbour. Then, having picked up more oars, the crew made two hazardous journeys through the broken water, and took on board the full crew of each ship in turn.

Already in 1866 the lifeboat was deemed unfit for further service. The cost of the new boat was paid by the inhabitants of Rochdale, in Lancashire, through the efforts of Mr. Robert Taylor Heape. The boat, built for the RNLI at a Limehouse yard, was delivered at Rochdale and exhibited there. It was named *Rochdale and Catherine Rashleigh* as a gesture to the donors of the first lifeboat, the Hon. Mrs. Rashleigh and William Rashleigh, of Menabilly, Fowey.

About eight thousand people turned out at Rochdale to see the boat as it was taken in procession through the town to Hollingforth Lake where, manned for the occasion by the crew of the Blackpool lifeboat, it was launched. On arrival at its destination in Cornwall the lifeboat was publicly launched from Par Sands. The station was eventually transferred to Fowey, three miles away.

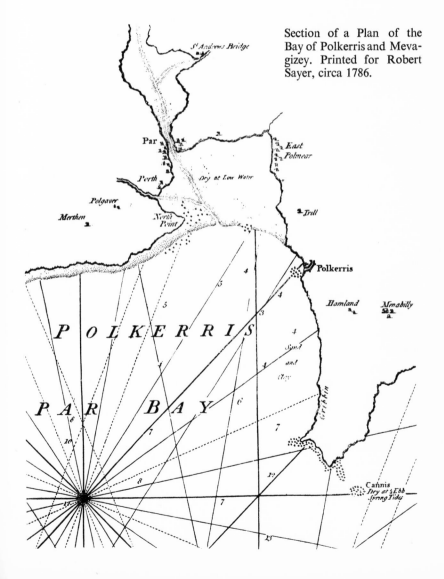

Section of a Plan of the Bay of Polkerris and Mevagizey. Printed for Robert Sayer, circa 1786.

CHARLESTOWN

IN the second half of the eighteenth century St. Austell, situated half way between Plymouth and Penzance on the ancient route through the south of Cornwall, became the centre of a mining district which, during the next hundred years or so was to produce large quantities of copper ore and refined tin. About 1775 the production of china clay and china stone began, and these materials were shipped in increasing quantities to the Staffordshire potteries. By the year 1800 the village had become a busy mining town, the most important of the county's Stannary headquarters, and a tin smelting centre with three "blowing houses" using charcoal as fuel. Shortly afterwards it acquired a modern smelting house using coal, and two iron foundries.

A little tin streaming had been carried on for centuries, but this new activity in metalliferous and china clay mining was something altogether different. Well before 1800 the nearby Polgooth tin mine was about the largest in Cornwall, and during the first thirty years of the nineteenth century important copper mines were opened in the district.

This fast expanding mining centre had no secure seaport, and all the supplies that were brought in for the mines—they nearly all came by sea—had to be unloaded at two beaches. Horse-drawn waggons and strings of mules carried away inland the cargoes of the Welsh colliers, the Scandinavian timber ships, and of those bringing iron, hemp, limestone and general hardware.

It fell to Charles Rashleigh, a mining adventurer, to construct the secure harbour that was badly needed. The industrial epoch in Cornwall threw up many men who carried out big engineering jobs that were awkward and complicated enough to make us wonder how they did it. Rashleigh had no bulldozers, mechanical excavators, rock-drilling machinery or teams of back-room boys to help him carve an artificial harbour out of the narrow rocky cove of West Polmear. Like J. T. Austin of

Par he was one of those many spirits of his time for whom no task was too formidable or too adventurous. Their problem was not money, although it would be if they were here to-day to carry out these tasks. They had to be of tough fibre, determined, ruthless, imaginative and of long and broad vision. And perhaps they would hardly have been men of their own era if they were not also stern taskmasters.

Rashleigh called in John Smeaton, the eminent engineer, to design the harbour, and the plans were approved. The ominous events in France that were shaking Europe did not deter Rashleigh. The work was begun in 1791 and took ten years to complete. As the main constructional work progressed Rashleigh set up the various adjunctive industries—rope-making, ship-building, lime burning, brick making and a pilchard fishery—and facilities demanded by the rapid increase in the trade of the new port.

West Polmear, renamed Charlestown after its creator, suffered scarcely any setback, as did many other Cornish ports, from the Napoleonic blockade. Its exports of copper ore soared, and there was enough trade of a general nature to justify the establishment of regular shipping lines to and from Bristol and London. Five locally owned sailing ships maintained these two services.

The china clay industry was already expanding fast well before the collapse of metalliferous mining in Cornwall. By 1850 Charlestown was shipping about fifteen thousand waggon loads of china clay a year, as well as a large tonnage of copper ore, and importing as much coal, timber and general merchandise as it could handle. All the china clay was sent away during the six months or so when it was dry enough to handle, but shipments were not always evenly spread out, and there were periods when over two hundred waggon loads a day were taken to the port. Not very much, but we are here back in the earlier Victorian era in a district without railways and full of difficult terrain. The parish roads got torn to pieces by the heavy waggons. At the foot of all the hills additional teams of horses were harnessed, and helped to haul the waggons to the top. There were over one hundred and fifty clay carriers in the district, nearly all of them farmers, for whom haulage work was a profitable sideline. For this reason farming properties close to china clay works were rated under the Poor Law higher than anywhere else: a curious phenomenon.

The expansion of the china clay industry was steady as well as rapid. More and more industries and markets found uses for this remarkable raw material. The output doubled itself twice between 1850 and 1900. By this date there was a good regular traffic between Charlestown and Viborg, Raumo, Abo, Gefle, Norrköping, Kotka and Riga, and also Gutujewski, the port for St. Petersburg. Danish sailing vessels had the Gutujewski trade. They usually returned to Charlestown loaded with barrel staves, which were used by the many thriving cooperages working for the china clay industry.

Regular cargoes went out from the port to Isigny, Nantes, La Pallice and, less frequently, to Cette (now Sète) and Libourne. The ships going to this inland port on the Dordogne river had to have a low air draught to let them pass under a bridge. These shipments to Libourne remind us of the river Fowey's trade with that port in the thirteenth century, when it was called Fozéra. It was founded by Henry III, and used as the distributing point for tin and cured fish exported to eastern Gascony.

Other ports served by Charlestown were Wormerveer, Zaandam, Dordrecht, Rotterdam and Amsterdam; Terneuzen (the Dutch port on the left bank of the Scheldt), Bruges, Ghent, Antwerp and Vilvorde (at one time the port for Brussels); Pasajes, Bilbao, Santander and Gijon.

The port's great days came to an end with the First World War, but it has continued to send away china clay regularly. To-day there are scarcely any imports, and no longer does such a variety of foreign ports appear in the charter-parties of vessels loading there.

PENTEWAN

FOR centuries small ships and barges carried away much fine building stone from the Duchy of Cornwall freestone quarry, which was situated barely half a mile from the beach. It was used very largely in church reconstruction in the late Middle Ages, and for substantial private residences in later periods.

In the mining era of the eighteenth century ships were often beached at Pentewan, bringing in supplies for the mines and taking away some of the mining produce. Then between 1820 and 1826 Sir Christopher Hawkins, a typical mining and political adventurer of the industrial era, built an artificial harbour under the cliffs. He had his eye on the growing china clay industry, which needed a harbour more accessible than Charlestown.

A railroad was then laid down linking Pentewan with St. Austell, a few miles to the north, to facilitate the carriage of china clay:

"At first when the waggons were loaded at St. Austell, they were set in motion by men who pushed them until they obtained enough speed on the slight down gradient to take them about two miles. When they reached level ground a horse pulled the waggons to the docks at Pentewan, where sailing ships were waiting for their cargoes."

This rapturous state of affairs, cheap and practical, if slow, went on for about forty years. Then steam locomotives were introduced.

Large quantities of silt and sand, first from the tin-streaming works up the valley, and then from the china clay works, were brought down by a fast running stream, gradually choking up the navigable channel outside the harbour. Just before the 1914 war one of the "Rose" steamers of Richard Hughes, the Liverpool ship-owner, got neaped at Pentewan for a fortnight. The channel was too shallow to allow the ship to get out. The port never recovered from the effects of this unfortunate news, and ships kept away from it.

Pentewan, never a happy or successful port, died a natural death soon after the First World War. The sandbank that was formed and pushed back the sea is now a site for caravans.

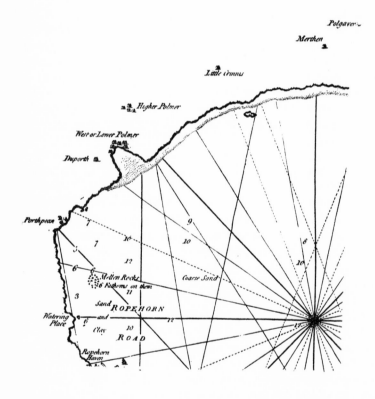

Section of a Plan of the Bay of Polkerris and Mevagizey.   Printed for Robert Sayer, circa 1786, showing West or Lower Polmer (Charlestown).

MEVAGISSEY

FOLLOWING the medieval custom the lord of the manor erected the first stone pier for the protection of the local fishing boats. This was between 1430 and 1480, when the idea of building such harbour works gained ground and was put into effect at several Cornish fishing villages. The same original pier was standing when in 1740 a survey of St. Austell Bay took note of its existence.

In the eighteenth century Mevagissey, benefiting from the general expansion of the Cornish fisheries—which ran parallel with the mining and industrial expansion—emerged as the fourth largest centre of the pilchard industry. It cured its pilchards for export to the Italian market, and from 1750 onwards it shipped about thirty-five millions of these fish a year.

Very soon the harbour could no longer accommodate the growing number of fishing vessels using it, and under an Act of Parliament of 1775 a new pier was built. Many cottages were adapted to the needs of the flourishing fishery, and room had to be found for the storage of more and more nets, tackle, barrels of cured pilchards awaiting shipment, pilchard oil and curing salt. Large curing cellars were erected right against the quay-sides. The village streets were narrow even for Cornwall, and some of them were not wide enough to allow the passage of loaded pack animals. Hence the rare sight—yet common enough at Mevagissey—of men in pairs, one behind the other, with large baskets of pilchards slung from poles carried on their shoulders.

Mevagissey's trade was crippled by the Napoleonic blockade, and with the traditional Italian market closed it found a new but only temporary outlet for its pilchards in the West Indies. With only Russian ports remaining open to British shipping during the blockade, Mevagissey turned to that source for supplies of hemp, tallow, iron and other materials for the mines and its own fishery. And it went to North America for the large quantities of barrel staves for its pilchard hogsheads.

With the revival of the fisheries in 1816 Mevagissey fitted out thirty pilchard seines, and thereafter thrived as never before. By 1850 no less than eighty fishing vessels of all types were registered at the port, giving employment to just over three hundred fishermen, packers and bulkers, and to ten fish-curing businesses.

Like every port on the Cornish coast Mevagissey built its own fishing boats, and between 1855 and 1875, the most active period of west country schooner building, it also launched several merchant schooners.

Under an Order-in-Council of 1866 Mevagissey, like its rivals Newlyn and St. Ives, was authorised to borrow a limited amount of capital at a low rate of interest for the purpose of improving its harbour facilities. A new outer pier was erected, increasing the area of the tidal harbour from three and a half to ten acres.

To-day this age-old village carries on a much reduced fishery with about twenty vessels. Its seaborne commerce has gone. A small coaster in 1950 brought in a cargo of Spanish salt, but that has been the only importation of any kind since the war. In that year an attempt was made to introduce new blood into the port's fishing industry by settling there a small group of Spanish fishermen, but the venture was not successful.

Mevagissey was a lifeboat station from 1869 to 1930. The first lifeboat, named *South Warwickshire*, was a gift of people in that county. Answering its very first call the lifeboat was thrown up on the shore immediately it was launched. After it was re-launched it had to be rowed into the teeth of a tremendous gale. The lifeboatmen rescued the crew of a sailing vessel of Bordeaux. The seamen were clinging to the rigging of their ship, which was a wreck. In a painstaking and dangerous operation, during which the lifeboat was constantly thrown about by the surf alongside the wreck, the seamen were taken on board one by one. The lifeboat was then beached on Par Sands, its crew exhausted from cold, exposure and fatigue. When manning their lifeboat to save the lives of others the fishermen of Mevagissey took risks—without making any calculation—in raging seas that they would never dare negotiate in the course of their normal occupation.

GORRAN HAVEN

THIS is yet another of the ancient fishing villages of Cornwall that has turned its back on the sea to cater for the holiday-makers.

In 1270 Bishop Bronescombe appropriated Gorran Church—a mile away in the village of Gorran—to the Glasney Collegiate Church at Penryn, which took the tithe of the seine nets and of all the seine boats in Gorran parish above the number of twelve. This is one of the earliest known references to seine fishing. This method of fishing can without much doubt be related to the trade in cured fish to Gascony at the opening of the thirteenth century. Seining yielded greater quantities of pilchards and mackerel than could be consumed locally, whether fresh or cured. For the fishermen of Gorran Haven it was but a short step across the bay to the Fowey river, where merchants of Bayonne in the thirteenth century came to pick up the cured fish and tin which they shipped to Oléron and the south-west of France.

At Gorran Haven stands the original chapel erected by the lord of the manor in the fifteenth century. The first small protective pier was built at the same time. The art of building really adequate piers belonged to the industrial era in Cornwall, when ample capital and a high degree of engineering skill made such projects an easier task. But medieval piers of the type built at Gorran Haven had to be good enough in their day, although they undoubtedly suffered damage in severe gales.

Lacking a hinterland Gorran Haven was destined for a stagnant existence. Much of its little merchandise was brought there by lighter after transhipment at Fowey. "A place much frequented by ships, boats, barges and lighters," wrote the historian Penaluna in 1808, "for fishing and carrying and re-carrying fish, goods and merchandise."

The old medieval pier was rebuilt soon after 1820, and in 1888 this second pier was reconstructed. There will be no need to rebuild it again, since it serves no purpose.

ST. MAWES

SITUATED just inside the broad Fal estuary St. Mawes was too exposed to attack to become a commercial fishery centre in the Middle Ages. But time brought changes, and by 1536 it had a stone pier, which could only have been put there for the protection of its fishing boats. The village grew with the building of the castle or fortress, which was begun in 1542 and was designed to defend the Fal ports from attack. In another twenty years St. Mawes achieved the distinction of sending two representatives to Westminster, a privilege that was retained until the passing of the Reform Act of 1832. The corporation itself was dissolved under the provisions of the Municipal Corporations Act of 1835.

St. Mawes lived by its fisheries, supplying much of Falmouth's exports of cured pilchards to Italy. It also occupied itself with the river Fal pilotage service, a large number of pilots working from there.

Under an Act of Parliament of 1854 the St. Mawes Pier and Harbour Company improved the pier and the harbour anchorage.

To-day St. Mawes is one of the loveliest and most restful places on the south coast of England, a jewel in a green and azure setting.

TRURO

HALF way between the north and south coasts Truro stands at the head of a main tidal creek of the Fal estuary. Like most medieval seaports, it was founded and grew up at the lowest point where its river could be bridged or forded. Truro is probably the oldest of the post-Norman Cornish seaports. Since commerce and industry alone brought medieval towns into existence, Truro can attribute its origin to the proximity of tin-streaming activities and to the need of a tin market, as well as of a seaport for the shipment of the refined metal.

Richard de Luci, Justiciar of the realm, was granted, in recognition of his services to Henry II, many estates in Cornwall, amongst them the manor of Kenwyn, on which part of Truro now stands. Although de Luci's charter for Truro has not survived, Ballard and Tait assign it to the year 1156. Reginald Earl of Cornwall, in renewing the charter in 1166, referred to the privileges granted by de Luci. A second renewal by Henry II between 1175 and 1189 confirmed to "the burgesses of Richard de Luci of Truro all the liberties and free customs which Earl Reginald my uncle gave them".

It would be unreasonable to ignore the indirect connection between Truro's first charter and that granted to Bordeaux— also its first—in the same year 1156 by Henry II. Both places had a close interest in the revived tin trade, which provided the Crown with much revenue. By 1160 Truro was undoubtedly shipping a little of the tin that was being produced in Cornwall and finding its way to the south-west of France and the north of Spain. The metal reached these places by way of the international market on the island of Oléron. Difficult to explain is Truro's omission as a seaport from the returns to the Winchester Assize of Customs in 1205; it means that the port had no dutiable imports or exports. It may have shipped some tin, but this commodity, being exempt from the duty, was excluded from the returns.

From 1224 until 1235 there are frequent references to official government business in maritime matters—the sequestering of ships and so on—in the Fal river. In every instance the records speak of the "port of Falmouth", but no inhabited place of that name existed until the seventeenth century. The term was applied to every trading point in the estuary, and until Penryn obtained its first charter the only enfranchised borough and authorised trading settlement in the river was Truro. In this early period we know that vessels of Bruges and of English ports were involved in incidents at "Falmouth", but whether they had come in for trade or merely to shelter no one can tell.

Truro prospered in the undisturbed quiet that prevailed in the west country in the long reign of Henry III, when tin mining, agriculture and the fisheries made much progress. In September 1259 Bishop Bronescombe performed three ceremonies in the town: the re-dedication of the enlarged church of St. Kenwyn, the dedication of the new chapel of St. Mary, and the consecration of the new church of the Friars Preachers of the Dominican Order. The Friars established themselves only in the larger centres of population in order to preach the faith to the poorest people. Undoubtedly Truro was growing.

In 1265 Richard Earl of Cornwall, on his release from prison, obtained from the King letters of safe conduct for "his merchants" of Truro, prior to their departure for La Rochelle and Bordeaux, to sell there the tin they had bought from him. Earl Richard, as King of the Romans, granted many privileges to German merchants, and about the year 1265 a merchant representing the Hanseatic towns of Lubeck and Hamburg was established at "Falmouth", most likely engaged in the production or buying of tin. This commodity was being regularly shipped from Cornwall to the depots of these two Hanses at Houcke and Oostkerke in Flanders.

In 1295 Truro, together with Helston, Bodmin, Lostwithiel and Liskeard, sent representatives to Westminster, not, as is often supposed, as members of Parliament, but merely to be consulted by the Council on matters concerning tin mining. The five boroughs were the recognised centres of the industry—although at this time Lostwithiel was the sole staple—and their delegates went to London only to contribute first-hand knowledge on the industry and its production as a source of revenue to the Crown. It was not by chance that in the following year, 1296, the whole output of tin in Cornwall was bought up by Edward I for re-sale at a profit. He did this largely to keep his Bayonne creditors quiet.

In the fourteenth century the trade of Truro and Penryn taken together seems, from the incomplete information contained in the customs records, to have been equal to about one-third of that done by the river Fowey ports. It was not until the sixteenth century, when Truro had superseded Bodmin and Lostwithiel as the main centre of the tin mining industry, that its seaborne trade became relatively important. Meanwhile it was conspicuous enough to draw attention to itself, for in 1377 and again in 1404 it suffered severe raids by the French. The first attack resulted in the town's "destruction", that is, its storehouses were looted and the ships lying in the port taken away or sunk. In the second raid it was set on fire.

By 1575 Truro was assaying and coining a third of all the tin mined and smelted in the county. While Lostwithiel, Bodmin, Liskeard and Launceston, the prosperous medieval boroughs farther east, were in full decline, Truro was in the ascendant. Both tin mining and shipping interests had moved westwards. The town now had many wealthy merchants, and more and more ships were attracted by the commerce it could offer. They came mainly from Rouen, La Rochelle, Oléron, Bilbao, London and other home ports.

We find Truro merchants going into the outside carrying trade in the Tudor period, hiring out ships on charter. Their vessels carried such consignments as "cottons" (woollen fabrics) from Carmarthen to Brittany, from Cardiff to La Rochelle; wine from Bordeaux to Tenby; salt from La Rochelle to Haverfordwest; and coal from Swansea to many ports in the south-west of England. This kind of trade—invisible exports—enriched the town and consolidated its position in the county.

The new town and port of Falmouth, created in the seventeenth century, took away some of Truro's commerce, but the corporation of the ancient city, if as a formality they opposed the Killigrew plan to build a town where Falmouth now stands, knew that Truro had little hope of stopping the tide of progress. Ships were getting larger and drawing more water, and only small sailing craft could reach Truro fully loaded. As a port it could do little more than hold on; as a mining and manu- facturing centre it still had a future.

Indeed, in the Georgian period Truro was looked upon as the metropolis of Cornwall. Over a long period many families had accumulated fortunes from mining, shipping and commerce— the Robartes, Vincents, Gregors, Lemons and Vivians amongst them. All the cultural characteristics and taste of Georgian civilisation began to appear. Fine houses and mansions were built in the woods and parklands around the town, and in Truro itself many substantial houses were erected and spacious streets laid out, a few of them, quite exceptionally for Cornwall, paved with sidewalks. A first-class public library was founded in 1792; a weekly newspaper in 1801, and the Royal Institution of Cornwall in 1818. This institution was established for the promotion of knowledge in natural history, archaeology, ethnology and the fine arts, and for the encouragement of literature. It was all something quite new for what was looked upon as the most retarded county in England.

Truro had a paper mill, a very large carpet factory, two potteries, a tannery, an iron foundry, tin smelting works and shipbuilding yards. Although no longer an important seaport it still had some shipping interests, and in the 1820s some thirty sea-going vessels were registered there. It was still sending tin to Russia, France, the Mediterranean lands and other countries, and copper ore to South Wales. It imported coal, iron, groceries, timber and general hardware. A common sight at Truro was large teams of horses hauling away from the quays and through the main streets specially built low waggons bearing enormous plunger poles for the mines in the vicinity.

The borough of Truro holds as one of its maces a miniature silver oar, the symbol of its jurisdiction over the whole Fal river in the Middle Ages. The port embraced all trading points as far as Mylor, close to Falmouth, and they included Newham

Looe   (Aerofilms & Aero Pictorial Ltd.)

The seal of East Looe   The seal of West Looe

Polperro, once a thriving fishing village   (*Western Morning News*)

Fowey, still a trading port after 800 years   (*Western Morning News*)

Quay; Calenick, where there were important tin smelting works; Malpas, which built ships and traded mainly in timber and oysters; Round Wood Quay; Tresillian, at the head of its muddy creek, and Devoran. This unique port was created expressly to serve the mines a few miles to the north-west, and a railroad was put down in 1826 for the transportation of copper ore, and of coal, timber and other supplies. The line reached Redruth and Chacewater in the country thick with active mines. Near Devoran stands the Norway Inn, named in the days of the port's prosperity, when large quantities of timber from Norway were discharged on the quays. There exists no better description of this short-lived and completely vanished port than that written by Basil Greenhill, who went there in search of the hulks of old sailing ships:

"Its quays stretched from the sluice by the main Falmouth-Truro road for nearly a mile downstream, granite edged quays paved and packed underneath with gravel. Buried deep in this gravel were granite bollards. Warehouses and engine sheds backed the quays and at the head of the river below the village was a system of small docks, each with its sheds and cranes, the sides of their entrance channels lined with heavy wooden posts joined and reinforced with iron bolts an inch in diameter. The ruins of this vanished harbour can plainly be seen to-day, the quays sunk into gravel banks with stray granite blocks and the tall pillars of the round bollards, standing naked to their original level, embedded in them. The gaunt frames of wooden steps rise from the water to the level of the paved quays that are no longer there. The sheds and warehouses are overgrown with bushes, and the silted docks, each a shallow, quite secluded pool, are the homes of shy water birds. You can follow the track of the old railway that ran down from the mines . . . And in the old docks, and on the banks below the ruined quays, and out in the shallow bed of the creek, that for forty years has not been dredged to take the deep hull of a laden schooner, lie the skeletons of old vessels. . . ."

Devoran exported the produce of the mines, and imported

pit props, coal and limestone. Two locally owned steamers worked regularly in and out of the port. Barges, the trading smacks of the Fal river, were built at various places on the banks of the creek.

Although all its small member ports and trading points have long ceased to carry on waterborne trade, Truro itself is visited by coasters bringing in coal, timber, cement, potatoes and so on. They are able to reach the quays in the town at spring tides.

Percy Upton   TRURO RIVER OYSTER BOAT

PENRYN

PENRYN, at the head of a tidal creek in the Fal estuary, and only about two miles to the north of Falmouth, was founded by Simon de Apulia, the Italian Bishop of Exeter, in the year 1216.

Under the patronage of the Bishops of Exeter, who held a manor there, the place grew and prospered. The first charter of enfranchisement, obtained in 1236, was renewed in 1259. The place was granted a weekly market and an annual fair. Soon afterwards Bishop Bronescombe founded the Glasney Collegiate Church at Penryn, endowing it with the patronage and tithe of sixteen parish churches. By 1308 the manor, with an important market, four corn mills and a fulling mill, was the most valuable of all the many temporalities of the bishops in Cornwall, rendering annually an amount equivalent to about £4,500 in terms of modern currency.

As a seaport Penryn had very little trade in the fourteenth century. It occurs jointly with Truro, under the name of Falmouth, in the customs returns of the Duchy, which do not reveal very much, since the parva custuma that was introduced in 1303 was levied on foreign merchants only; hence the foreign trade of English merchants and all coastwise trade by them went unrecorded. Barley, wheat, garlic, tallow, wine and fish-curing salt were amongst its imports, and cheese and tin (most of this commodity illegally) were exported.

The administration of maritime law to passing mariners and seaborne merchants seems to have been the responsibility of the bishop, who held the franchise and acted through his bailiff or steward. The borough of Truro had jurisdiction in maritime matters over the whole of the Fal estuary with the exception of the creek under the control of the Bishop of Exeter, a curious anomaly that was yet quite typical of medieval contradictions.

Before the construction of the forts at St. Mawes and on Pendennis Head at the mouth of the Fal in the sixteenth century the estuary was wide open to attack. French and Spanish ships —war vessels, privateers and pirates alike—made a habit of prowling off the Cornish coast. Penryn and Truro were both places worth looting, and indeed this fate twice befell Truro. One of the bishops, probably Stafford, therefore felt justified in building defences at Penryn. Leland, Henry VIII's surveyor and topographer, wrote of these defences in 1536:

> "Stakes and foundation of stone sette in the creeke at Penrine, afore the toun, a little lower than wher it brekith into armes. A gap in the middle of the stakes and a chain."

In other words a boom across the entrance. The collegiate church was "strongly wallid and incastellid, having 3 strong towers and gunnes at the but of the creeke".

Leland also stated that Penryn was "a prety town of marchandyse and vytayle market". In his time the word pretty meant "considerable".

Penryn was in fact one of the principal ports on the English Channel coast for the victualling of ships. After London, the Fal river in the Tudor period and for three centuries afterwards saw more shipping than any other port in the realm. Some of the visiting ships came for trade; many to shelter from unfavourable weather or contrary winds; a few arrived or left with ambassadors, royalty, king's messengers and so on, to be spared the sea journey up or down the Channel; the majority however, made the Fal a port of call, the last if outward bound, the first if homeward bound, to replenish their supplies of water and food.

Medieval trading ships remained in port from a few to several weeks, to enable their merchants to negotiate their business, sell their wares and buy their outward cargoes at the neighbouring weekly markets. Supplies of water and provisions had to be obtainable during the long sojourns in port. With many ships coming in for their various purposes—trade, provisions and security in bad weather—we see why Penryn already in 1308 had four active corn mills, a very high number for so small a manor.

Penryn was also important to seamen in that it ministered spiritual comfort. A chantry certificate of the year 1552 recited of Glasney that ships "have allwayes used to resort to the saide Colledge to se the mynystracon there . . .".

In the seventeenth century change was comparatively rapid; there was progress and a stronger sense of purpose in the air. Especially important was the increase in mining activity. More trade came to the Fal river, and the new town and port of Falmouth were created to deal with much of it. But Penryn survived and was still busy. Much the same sort of commerce was carried on at both ports. They were also entrepôts, re-exporting tobacco imported from Virginia, "Manchester" wares, hardware and Welsh coal. A typical general cargo that left Penryn for Maryland in 1696 consisted of woollen stockings, 2,880 tobacco pipes, pewter, woollen rugs, bays wear (?), British linen, fustians, painted calicoes, Spanish wine, conger and herrings. In the same year a typical cargo for Spain was made up of coal, lead, tin, pewter, beeswax, butter and tobacco. Like the cargo for Maryland, only part of it was of Cornish origin.

A good normal inward cargo from London consisted of soap, boxes of copper farthings, drapery, spirits, deals, chairs, tin wares, leather, ironwares, grindlestones, pitch, tar, oil and groceries. Frequent cargoes of charcoal for tin smelting came in from Southampton, while regular consignments of tin went to Plymouth and London.

Penryn was destined to handle much of the lucrative trade of the vast number of mines between the river and Redruth, and it was not until the late 1820s that this was lost to the new port of Devoran. In this mining era Penryn imported timber from Norway and Ireland, iron castings from Birmingham (shipped via Bristol), coal from South Wales, and foodstuffs from Ireland to help nourish the growing mining population.

Then came the granite trade. By the early part of the nineteenth century Penryn was shipping wrought and scabbled granite for dockyard and other constructional works at home and abroad. The Fastnet lighthouse, the old Waterloo Bridge, the pedestal of a monument in Turin, the Scutari memorial to the dead of the war in the Crimea, Billingsgate market and Waterford Cathedral were some of the works in which Penryn granite, sometimes as well as granite from other sources, was employed.

It was Henry Swann of Esher, Surrey, one of the members of Parliament for Penryn from 1806 to 1826, who procured the contract for the supply of granite for Waterloo Bridge. Nick-named the Black Swan, he was involved with his fellow Member of Parliament for Penryn, Sir Christopher Hawkins, in charges of corruption. Penryn in this period suffered from, or perhaps it would be more accurate to say enjoyed, ill-fame throughout the land as one of the most corrupt of Cornwall's "rotten boroughs". But it was still an epoch of swashbuckling adven-ture, when money so smoothly achieved what all other forms of persuasion failed to do. Penryn worked hard and played hard. Drinking, gambling and fervent Methodism all flourished side by side. It was a wonderful epoch for the busy little industrial and seaport town.

The merchants and shipowners of Penryn used six sailing ships of their own on the regular service to and from London; two others traded with Plymouth and two more again with the Isle of Wight. It was a commendable effort for such a small place to have so many ships operating its own cargo lines.

The town had plenty of small industries to keep its quays full of shipping. There was the cutting and dressing of granite from more than fifty quarries in the district; there were flour, paper and saw mills, a tannery, a chemical manure works and, not the least important, engineering and iron works casting stamp heads for ore-crushing and making other mining equipment.

Many shipbuilding yards in the vicinity turned out a large number of schooners. Some of these ships traded coastwise, some went into the ocean traffic to Newfoundland and South America, a few specialised in the granite trade, and others were fitted with water tanks and ventilated holds for the Corunna-Penryn cattle run. At the most these ships could carry some sixty head of cattle. The fast vessels were excellent for the job, and with a following wind they could sometimes reach Penryn within fifty hours of sailing from Corunna. Occasionally, when the winds were contrary, the animals were in poor shape on disembarkation. They got talked about, and this led to the

Plan of Falmouth and Carreg Road. Printed for Robert Sayer, c. 1786.

▶

traffic being stopped after a brief run of some twenty-five years.

Early in the 1870s the borough acquired from the Ecclesiastical Commissioners for a consideration of £10,000 the foreshore that had been part of the thirteenth century episcopal manor. To-day the port is in an advanced state of decline, although it does carry on a little seaborne trade.

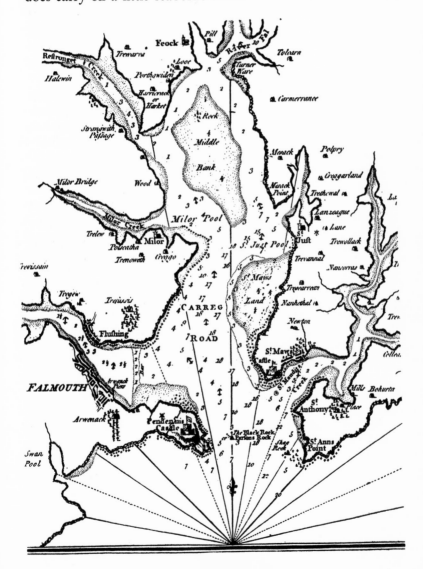

FALMOUTH

ONE of the finest natural harbours in the British Isles, and certainly the most fortunate in its situation, Falmouth, standing at the entrance to the world's busiest shipping channel, has always been used as a port of refuge and often as a port of call. During the long centuries of sailing ships it was well placed for weather-bound vessels waiting to set out, whether it was for the Irish Sea, the Atlantic Ocean, the Bay of Biscay, or eastwards up the Channel.

In medieval documents the "port of Falmouth" occurs repeatedly, yet no inhabited place of that name existed until the seventeenth century. The name of the river was used to designate all the trading points on its tidal waters.

The construction by Henry VIII of the two fortresses guarding the entrance to the Fal meant that there was something worth defending. Indeed, in the Tudor period more shipping was frequenting the river for various purposes than any other port on the south coast of England.

This new era of rapidly expanding trade was also one of intensive privateering. Even many unofficial privateers, not formally commissioned but officially victualled and armed, and manned to some extent by mixed crews of English seamen and French protestant refugees, used the Fal as their base. Their actions were against not only French ships, but also those of several papist countries, and occasionally English vessels. French, Portuguese, Spanish and Dutch ships were often detained at Falmouth for long periods before the government authorised the release of those that could not legally be seized. It mattered little whether they were arrested at sea or came in under the stress of weather.

Early in the seventeenth century the Killigrews of Arwenack manor agitated repeatedly for permission to build a town at the hamlet of Smithwick, and in the end, after much opposition, mainly from Penryn, Truro and Helston, succeeded in obtaining the consent of the government. The Killigrew plan included the building of a new Custom House to replace the old one at

Penryn. It was erected near the quay which Sir John Killigrew had built and to which he brought a piped water supply for the use of shipping and of the inhabitants.

At last on 20th August 1660 the name of Smithwick was changed to Falmouth, and in the next year a charter of incorporation was obtained. The new corporate body were not too happy about this Killigrew creation. The burgess members of the corporation were largely local merchants who naturally wanted for themselves a good share of the profits and perquisites arising from the increasing amount of trade the Killigrews had brought to the town. In deference to the wishes of certain members the corporation passed a by-law imposing arbitrary fines on newcomers opening a business at Falmouth, a measure that allowed them to discriminate against anyone they did not approve. A maker of shoes, for instance, was heavily fined, and when a Killigrew intervened on his behalf the newcomer was warned that he would get no peace and would be ruined if he remained at Falmouth. Such were the jealousies and growing pains of the young corporation.

Under the national customs system Falmouth and Penryn were treated as one port, and it is not possible to determine the share of the joint trade handled by each. It was probably about the same. We find their commerce steadily increasing in the latter part of the seventeenth century, more and more cargoes going to foreign and colonial destinations: Roscoff, St. Malo, Rouen, Nantes, La Rochelle, Bordeaux, Bayonne, Madeira, Newfoundland, Virginia, Venice, Leghorn, Bilbao, Cadiz, Alicante, Tunis and "The Straights", then, but now no longer, signifying the "Straights" of Gibraltar.

Imports came mainly from the French Atlantic ports and St. Malo, "Drounton", "St. Martons", Bilbao, Lisbon, Naples, Amsterdam, Malmoe, Bergen, Virginia, Antigua ... Although Falmouth's trade was largely of an international character its coastwise shipping was also important, the numbers of arrivals and departures being only slightly less than those engaged in the foreign and colonial traffic. Then there were also the many unrecorded ships that came in for water, provisions or merely to shelter from bad weather.

In 1688 Falmouth was first appointed as a Post Office Packet Station, and within a few years it became the leading such establishment in the country, surpassing those which served the Baltic lands, Holland and Ireland.

At first the Packets carried the Post Office mails to and from Corunna only; a little later a service was opened to Lisbon. Then followed the West Indies and North America, and by about 1760 there were routes to Bermuda, Jamaica and other islands, to New York, Pensacola, Charleston, Savannah and St. Augustine (Florida). Soon afterwards further services were inaugurated to Halifax, Vera Cruz, Tampico, Surinam, Brazil and Buenos Aires. The number of ships performing the services was always varying; in 1782 eighteen vessels were employed on the Caribbean and North American routes, and by 1827 some forty Packets were based at Falmouth. When the new steam vessels came into use after 1830 half a dozen of them were taking the mails to and from Vigo, Oporto, Lisbon, Gibraltar, Malta, Greece and the Ionian Islands, Egypt and the remote East Indies.

The increasing use of the steamship meant that Falmouth had a poor future before it as the main Packet Station, and Southampton took its place. By 1850 every one of the Falmouth services had been transferred there. But for some one hundred and fifty years the Falmouth Packets contributed a very creditable chapter to the nation's maritime history.

The ships were small neat brigantines designed for speed. In the not infrequent periods of war they were armed with cannon for defensive purposes, and carried crews of forty to fifty men, including a surgeon, as compared with only twenty-five to thirty men in peace time.

These little ships had always of course to contend with the Atlantic storms, and some of them disappeared without leaving a trace, but in times of war and of uneasy peace they often had to fight their way to their destinations. Always, without exception, they were up against stronger opposition, encountering privateers in groups of perhaps three or four, each of them more heavily armed than the Packets, and manned by crews of rarely less than ninety to a hundred. Some brilliant

victories were gained by the Packets, but many of them were
sunk or captured.

All through the eighteenth century, almost without interruption, French privateers harassed English shipping in the English
Channel, whilst the notorious Algerian pirates sometimes
caused havoc off the Cornish coast, capturing ships and
carrying off their crews and passengers to North Africa into
slavery. If the Packets were occasionally disturbed by these
prowlers at the western end of the Channel, their regular enemies were to be found far out in the Bay of Biscay and in the
West Indies, where the main French base was Guadeloupe.
And in the second American war which began in 1812 the
Falmouth Packets would run into American frigates and
privateers almost anywhere. They suffered heavy losses from
these ships. The period of the Napoleonic wars and the Continental System was one of almost continuous fighting for the
Packets.

The Falmouth vessels fought thirty-two actions in the three
years of hostilities from 1812 to 1814, winning seventeen
victories against aggressors superior in manpower and guns, but
losing heavily in men and ships. Some of the Packets captains
had outstanding ability, and were good tacticians, possessing as
well a flair for leadership in emergencies. Their vessels were not
ships of war, but mail boats, and their orders were not to use
their guns unless they were first attacked. And if they were
attacked without a chance of winning or of escaping, they had to
sink the mails and strike their colours.

A brief account of one action will serve to illustrate the type
of incident that every Packet was likely to encounter on every
journey except in times of settled peace. When the acting
master of the Packet was killed and the mate seriously wounded
during an attack by a French privateer off Jamaica, the command of the ship fell to the boatswain, Richard Pasco. After
desperate hand to hand fighting and close musketry fire Pasco
and his little crew got the better of the enemy. He could have
let the privateer go, but he was not satisfied with a partial
victory. His blood was up, and he wanted to make a capture
of the aggressor. When he saw the two vessels beginning to

draw apart he sprang into the rigging, went up aloft and lashed the privateer's square-sail yard to the Packet's fore shrouds. Then for another half an hour he and his men kept up their fire and "made the enemy cry for mercy". When Pasco and his party boarded the privateer some of the surviving enemy crew jumped overboard, eventually getting drowned, since, having nailed their "bloody" flag to the masthead, they expected no quarter. Of the privateer's crew of sixty-five not less than thirty-two were found lying dead on the decks, and only sixteen were unhurt. Two of the Packet's crew were killed and several badly wounded.

Carriers of the Post Office mails, the Packets were unofficially also trading ships. James Silk Buckingham of Falmouth, whose father had been killed in an action when serving as master of a Packet, first went to sea on the Lisbon run when only nine years old. In his autobiography he said that every member of the crew from the captain to the galley boy was allowed space for some merchandise to sell at the port of destination. He himself took

"... a little trading stock of velveteens, muslins and other articles sure to find a ready sale in Lisbon ... Mercantile houses were established at Falmouth in correspondence with others in London, by whom were furnished every description of goods suited to the markets of the several ports to which the packets sailed. As the officers and crews of these packets were permanently employed, and most of them married and settled or belonging to families residing at Falmouth, they were all safe to be entrusted with any reasonable amount of goods on credit. ... It would often happen that the captain would take £5,000 worth of general goods, with watches and jewellery, the officers their £3,000 or £2,000 each, and the men frequently £1,000 or rarely less than £500 each on sale or return."

At Lisbon the goods were, by arrangement, "smuggled" ashore, the Customs officers and government and church officials sharing in the profits of this trade.

If, on their return, the Packets were exempt from Customs inspection, the goods brought home by the crews were still dutiable, and therefore had to be smuggled ashore. According to Buckingham the crews traded in

". . . Havannah segars, port wine, and other articles paying a high duty in England, which were again smuggled on shore, on the ship's arriving in the British Channel, either by the fishing and pilot boats from the Scilly Islands, Mount's Bay and the west coast of Cornwall, or after the ship had anchored, in night visits to the shore."

In the early part of the nineteenth century the private cargoes of the Packets, according to the Collector of the Customs at Falmouth, were worth over £4 million a year. Private trading by the crews of the West Indies Packets was forbidden when certain irregularities came to light, but when the ban was applied to the Lisbon Packets mutiny broke out. When the trouble was over the ban remained in force.

The Packets also carried passengers, the fares being a perquisite of the captains. It cost a passenger £23 to be taken to Lisbon, £38 to Gibraltar, £54 to New York and £107 to Brazil. It was expensive travel.

The Packets were always privately owned, sometimes by a group of shareholders, often by the captain. The vessels were hired by the Postmasters-General (the office was jointly held by two people) at an annual fee of £1,800 each.

Life was never dull at Falmouth in the eighteenth century. Something was always turning up, even if it was only bad weather driving ships in to shelter and their crews to spend their money. There were occasionally rumours and threats of invasion, press-gangs hunting for seamen, news of the fate of a Packet ship, arrivals and departures of naval flotillas, the sales of prize cargoes. . . . Anticipating the "approaching war" a Falmothian wrote in 1739:

"The Town seems to be in statu quo. Trade little, money scarce, a plenty of Smuggled Commodities, and a numerous poor. . . . There is something to be hoped, past experience teaching us that the Town will flourish in a French war . . ."

He was not the only cynic at Falmouth. Another one in 1743 had this to say:

"The Commissioners of the customs are making sad work among our Shopkeepers and Pacquets people, and seem Determined to break ye Neck of the trade carryed on in these things, which I apprehend will be an Ugly thing for the Falmouth people, this trade being ye Best Support of our Shopkeepers who send Great Quantities of Woollen Stockings, hatts, Pewter and other Goods . . . by ye Saylers for Sale . . ."

Then we read of three large East India merchant ships from China that were in port "drawing the Town and Country of all the loose money that can be scraped together." Hundreds of people flocked into Falmouth to buy the private cargo merchandise smuggled ashore by the officers and men of these ships. On another occasion a homeward bound East Indiaman was in port for a fortnight doing a brisk trade on board, although she was attended by two naval cutters and the Custom House boat.

Nothing could be done to check this type of open contraband traffic when men like Captain Isaac Cocart, a well-known smuggler, could twice hold office as mayor of Falmouth and sit as chief magistrate. From smuggling Cocart joined the Customs service and was appointed to a Custom House vessel which cruised off the coast in search of smugglers' ships. Cocart also did much business in Lisbon, using the Packet ships for the purpose.

Another prominent Falmouth merchant was Peter Hill, who died in 1743 worth £30,000 in "ready money", a neat little fortune at that period, which he had accumulated from shipchandlering.

A typical Falmothian was Theophilus Daubuz, a Huguenot refugee who came to the town about the year 1730. In 1744 he was appointed as a licensed privateer, but having made only two prizes in two months and "pillaged a little town on ye coast of Spain", making no more than £1,000, he settled down as a merchant and became rich.

During the greater part of the restless eighteenth century naval vessels were stationed in the harbour, and their job of protecting shipping entailed a great deal of patrol and convoy work. Extracts from the journal of Rear-Admiral Bartholomew

James give us a vivid description of the day-to-day routine of
one of many naval vessels based at Falmouth. This part of the
diary was written when James was first-lieutenant of H.M.
Sloop *Aurora*.

"... On 24 June we bore away for St. Mary's in Scilly.
Sailed thence 25 June and for 7 days cruised off and on in
Lat. 46° 30' and about 50 leagues to the westward of
Scilly ... On 1 July we anchored in Mts Bay. The 3rd we
sailed again ... in quest of a privateer.... July 9 we chased
a cutter all night, and on the 10th put into Milford in
Wales. ... On the 19th we put again into St. Ives and the
21st off the Lands End, chased a privateer brig sixteen
hours without success. ... On the 29th we sailed ... with
two tin ships for the Downs, where we arrived on August
1.... On September 1 we left Spithead, and on the 3rd, off
Portland in a calm, boarded and took a lugger smuggler
loaded with gin and tea; and on the 4th arrived with the
prize at Falmouth ... on the 11th ... came to sail ... with
a convoy bound to Bristol. ... The 11th sent the cutter in
chase of a brig which she retook, loaded with lead, having
been taken by a Dutch privateer. ... October 4th we sailed
... for Mts. Bay, where, taking under convoy four brigs,
two sloops and a schooner, we again put to sea ... and on
the 12th, meeting with a gale of wind, put into Plymouth
Sound, where on the 18th our convoy was increased to
eighty-three sail; and with which we proceeded to the
Downs, where we arrived on the 20th, having on our
passage retaken a brig from Swansea loaded with coals.
... On October 27th sailed ... with the *Kite* cutter and a
convoy for Portsmouth. On the 28th gave chase to a
cutter for six hours and lost her in the night. ..."

And so it went on with little respite week after week for
another four months until that particular period of hostilities
came to an end. There was plenty of work for the ships based
at Falmouth, and in addition to the smaller patrol vessels two
full squadrons of frigates were stationed there. The Admiralty
built a pier in Mylor Creek, mainly to facilitate the supply of
fresh water by lighter to ships of the navy.

Opposite Falmouth the little village of Flushing had been growing fast. It had quays but not a fraction of the trade it had hoped to take away from Falmouth itself. It was more of a residential place. During the Napoleonic period it enjoyed much prosperity from the social side of naval and maritime life. The village streets, according to an observer, "literally sparkled" with gold epaulets, gold lace hats and brilliant uniforms. The officers and seamen of the Packets were "handsome and well-dressed in uniforms". In proportion to its size Flushing saw "more of the gaiety and elegance of life" than any other place in England. There were dinners, balls and parties every evening, and three or four dances every night "at the more humble places of resort" for the sailors and their lasses.

Although its trade was relatively unimportant, Falmouth handled in the 18th and 19th centuries a great variety of merchandise and products. From France came wine, brandy, salt, grain, flour and fruit; from Russia, the Baltic lands and Germany hemp, pitch, tar, tallow, iron, sail-cloth, linen, grain and timber; from Holland cheese, Geneva (gin), grain and butter; from Spain and Portugal salt, wool, fruit, brandy and wine; from Ireland grain and other foodstuffs; from Merseyside salt, earthenware, coal and general hardware; from North America tobacco, barrel staves and timber, wheat, rice and flour; from South America wool, cotton, sugar and hides.

Falmouth's direct exports went to Italy, Malta, Turkey and other countries in the Mediterranean; France, the Netherlands, Germany and Russia; Spain and Portugal, and many English ports. They included tin, pilchards, pilchard oil, copper ore and a great amount of woollens, cottons, iron and general merchandise as re-exports.

It would not be an exaggeration to say that Falmouth was a dynamic seaport; for its size it was amazingly active. In 1822 America, Denmark, France, Hamburg, Hannover, Lübeck, Bremen, the Netherlands, Oldenburg, Prussia, Sweden, Norway, Russia, Portugal, Spain, Sicily and Sardinia were represented by vice-consuls there. This reflects the town's extensive commercial and shipping interests.

By the beginning of the nineteenth century Falmouth had

Par, Cornwall's busiest port   (Aerofilms & Aero Pictorial Ltd.)

Mevagissey   (Aerofilms & Aero Pictorial Ltd.)

Falmouth, with Penryn at the head of the creek   (*Aerofilms & Aero Pictorial Ltd.*)

Modern Falmouth   (*Western Morning News*)

become a port of call for orders, for both outward and homeward bound ships. The reason for calling there was that the masters and supercargoes of ships had to be kept informed of the state of the market to which they were bound. At Falmouth they received their final instructions as to their destinations, or they decided themselves to which port they would proceed for the disposal of their merchandise.

This practice of calling at Falmouth strengthened the existing system of sailing in convoys. Outward bound ships from the Clyde, Mersey and Severn ports would often call there, if not to receive orders, at least to join convoys. Very large assemblies were frequently to be seen in the harbour roads, and they were much larger still when ships were driven in under stress of weather. Probably the greatest number of ships ever there at one time was in 1815, when 350 vessels of all types rode out a succession of storms.

In the nineteenth century, Falmouth's golden age, it was a national as well as a regional port, and one of the best known in the world. As we have already seen, no port in the British Isles can have had such a variety of activities or filled so many roles as Falmouth. Until the nineteenth century passengers travelling to and from many parts of the world passed through it; it had an important ship-chandlering and victualling trade; it was a Post Office Packets Station; in some of our wars with continental countries it has served as a base for naval operations, and in the Second World War it launched the attack on the German-held naval base of St. Nazaire, and was also the headquarters of the exiled Royal Netherlands Navy; it has been a trooping port, a convoy assembly port, a port of refuge, a centre of the pilchard fishery, a lifeboat station, a general trading port; it has long been a base for ocean going tugs; it was a leading centre of the wooden schooner-building industry in the nineteenth century, and to-day it is one of the world's most important repair centres for tankers, passenger and cargo liners, and ocean tramps.

In 1872, an average year in the period of busiest shipping activity, three thousand nine hundred and forty-five ships entered Falmouth, proceeding to or from overseas destinations.

Less than half of them were British. In the same year almost as many ships in the coastwise trade entered the port, making a total of about seven thousand five hundred. The Trinity House pilotage receipts for Falmouth for the twelve months ending 30th September 1872 amounted to £15,065 19s. 8d., a figure exceeded only by the Port of London. Falmouth thus saw more shipping than Liverpool, Glasgow, Hull or Bristol.

By 1912 the number of ships using the port had fallen to about two thousand six hundred, although many of them were larger than those of some forty years earlier.

The fisheries of Falmouth and its member ports just before the outbreak of the First World War were flourishing. The number of fishing boats registered under Falmouth was one hundred and ninety-two, employing about seven hundred and thirty fishermen; these figures compare with eighty-five vessels and two hundred and three fishermen in 1850.

The busiest shipbuilding period ran from about 1850 to 1880, and there were many yards on the banks of the Fal and its creeks, each of them turning out from one to half a dozen wooden sailing ships a year. In the aggregate the number of ships launched in the area put Falmouth amongst the leading centres of schooner building in the British Isles.

Like Par, Padstow and Newquay, Falmouth specialised in the financing and managing of small sailing vessels. Groups of local people had interests in deep-water schooners that traded just about anywhere from Canada to Smyrna, and from St. Petersburg to the Argentine. Their vessels seem to have been the first to run in the fresh fruit traffic from Spain and the Central Mediterranean.

All this shipbuilding and merchant schooner trading has passed into history, but Falmouth has, as we have seen, gone into ship-repairing on a large scale. Sometimes more than a score of ships, totalling probably half a million registered tons, are in the docks under repair and overhaul or awaiting attention. The Falmouth Docks and Engineering Company have built a dry dock which, at the time of its construction, was the largest privately owned dock of its kind in the British Isles. It can receive ships of eighty-five thousand tons.

THE HELFORD RIVER

THE five miles of the navigable Helford River have seen ships coming and going, perhaps not continuously, but intermittently and probably at frequent intervals, ever since Roman times. Four camps of Roman type on its banks guarded the estuary. The Romans did not settle in Cornwall, but their merchants or factors came there for tin. Wherever there is archaeological evidence of ancient tin mining or smelting there are also found Roman coins and, usually not so far away, camps of Roman type. The Helford penetrates one of the districts rich in these finds.

Gweek, the medieval port for Helston, stands at the upper limit of the navigable waterway. It was a typical medieval contradiction of normal town development that the borough and tin coinage centre of Helston should be situated where it is, instead of at Gweek, the obvious site. It grew up closer to the rich tin grounds lying to the north. It acquired burgess privileges and a gild merchant in 1201. The commerce of its port was small, and coastwise only, for Gweek does not appear in the medieval national customs accounts, which recorded the customs paid only by foreign merchants.

Gweek came into its own in the Tudor period, which saw a great expansion in tin mining in the Helston district. Much charcoal for tin smelting had to be imported through the port, although charcoal pits in the woods along the banks of the Helford River continued to supply some of the fuel used by the tinners.

There were several trading points on the river. Merthen Quay, one of the nearest to Helston, was the highest point that could be reached by Norwegian ships that brought in timber during the great mining era of the eighteenth century. Their cargoes were unloaded into barges, which took the timber to the drying pool. Merthen had a good trade in oysters.

Further downstream were Scott's Quay, owing its existence to the Constantine granite trade of the nineteenth century, and Port Navas, the centre of the Helford oyster fisheries. There are still important oyster beds in the picturesque creek.

Opposite, on the right bank of the river, is Helford, once the busiest of the Helford trading places, where stood the custom house for the whole estuary. It dealt in agricultural produce, fertilisers, hardware and pilchards.

Gillan Harbour, near the mouth, occurs in late medieval port documents. It had its own ships trading to Southampton with cured hake, ling, "meluel", fish oil, hides and roofing slate. Later still, in the sixteenth century and after, ships of Gillan were engaged in the export trade in tin.

PORTHS OF THE
HUNDRED OF KERRIER

UNDER this title the group of fishing hamlets of the Lizard Peninsula were from 1337 onwards let at farm by the Duchy of Cornwall havener for the modest sum of 32/- a year— equivalent to about £100 to-day—but reduced after the Black Death pestilence to 25/-.

The porths included all the coves and beaches where a small commercial fishery was carried on, from Maen Porth just south of Falmouth, to Porthleven, in Mounts Bay, westward of Lizard Point. Gweek was apparently excluded since it was the recognised seaport of the enfranchised borough of Helston.

Porthallow and Porthoustock (pronounced Proustock), ancient porths, still had between them in 1850 a dozen registered fishing vessels. To-day roadstone is shipped from Porthoustock. During its period as a lifeboat station from 1869 to 1945 there were only thirty two launches.

Coverack, occurring as Porth Coverec in 1262, also remains the same unchanging place set amongst magnificent natural scenery. On a quiet summer's afternoon, with the hum of bees in the air, the curving bay of motionless azure water, seen through a small cluster of pines, has a delicate Mediterranean atmosphere.

The farmers of the Lizard district obtained their manure from such places as Coverack. The stuff consisted of damaged and decayed pilchards and curing salt condemned as unfit for further use. Saturated with rich pilchard oil this manure, mixed with sand and earth, produced crops of corn about 20 per cent better than the average.

Coverack has been a lifeboat station since 1901, and up to the end of 1955 161 lives had been saved.

A few miles further south in this holiday district is Cadgwith, formerly a fishing and smuggling cove. Its lifeboat station, opened in 1867, was closed down only in 1960. Nearly four hundred lives had been saved in eighty rescue operations.

Lizard Cove is, strictly speaking, two adjacent inlets under the cliffs, Polpeer and Penvoose. They were at one time the most southerly trading places in the British Isles, if also about the tiniest. Both lacked shelter, but the masters of the little colliers would beach their craft at the one which looked the safer in the wind that happened to be blowing when they got to the Lizard.

The Lizard lifeboat station was opened in 1859, and by the end of 1955 five hundred and fifty-two lives had been saved, the highest number by the lifeboatmen of any single station on the Cornish coast. Nowhere else in the British Isles were there three lifeboat stations on a six miles stretch of coast, as there were here—Coverack, Cadgwith and the Lizard—but nowhere else was there the same need for them, particularly in the days of sail. In 1960 a new station was built and opened at Polpeer Cove, supplanting the Cadgwith and the old Lizard stations.

Westward of the Lizard stands Mullion Cove amidst the most splendid and romantic coastal scenery in the British Isles. The cliffs are on a majestic scale, and from them one looks down on seagulls gliding far below on air currents. A light heat haze and a heavy ground swell add something indefinably magnificent to the whole scene. But in dirty weather the ugly dark broiling seas pounding against the massive rocks and cliffs can be almost terrifyingly mournful.

Mullion Cove turned to pilchard seining in the great expansion of the fisheries in the eighteenth century. Its seines were controlled by the big seining companies whose main interests were at the busier fishing ports. As Mullion had no cellars the pilchards were taken to Newlyn for curing and shipment to the Mediterranean.

The system of paying the seine fishermen was peculiar to Mullion. Each huer, in the 1870s, received 17/- a week plus every twentieth dozen of the fish caught. The two net shooters were paid 10/6d. a week each, plus one and a quarter shares each of 25 per cent of the whole catch, plus 2d. each on every hogshead (3,000 fish) of the seine owners' share of the catch. The master of the cock boat and the bowman received 9/- a week each, plus one and a quarter shares each of 25 per cent of the whole catch, plus 1d. each on every hogshead of the seine owners' share of the catch. The remaining members of the seine crews got 9/- a week each, plus a share each of 25 per cent of the whole catch.

In the nineteenth century Mullion tended to specialise more in crab and lobster fishing, each crabber working about 50 pots. The shell fish were rarely landed locally, but were gathered in time to be transferred to the Isles of Scilly ketch or smack which called every ten days or so to take them to Southampton.

Mullion Cove was also a lifeboat station for 41 years down to 1908, during which time it had only fourteen service calls.

The next place westwards on the Mounts Bay coast is Porthleven. Although only two miles from the ancient tin mining centre of Helston it never became its recognised port, since the entrance to the cove faced south-west, from which direction came the prevailing wind. Even a light wind and a moderate sea could make entry into the cove difficult.

In 1811 an Act of Parliament was obtained for the construction of an artificial harbour, the promoters being a group of London merchants who formed themselves into the Porthleven Harbour Company. The idea was said to have been prompted by humanitarian sentiments, with the intention to provide a secure harbour of refuge for wind-bound vessels forced to take shelter under that unfriendly shore of Mounts Bay.

The task proved to be far more costly than the ill-informed promoters had imagined, and amongst many onerous jobs to be carried out was the removal, mainly by manual means, of some 380,000 tons of mud and gravel. There was a great deal of mismanagement, and dissension amongst the promoters, before the work was finally completed in 1818. Some twenty years later Davies Gilbert, historian and sometime president of the Royal Society, wrote:

"... Porthleaven, heretofore a small fishing cove, till some projectors induced credulous persons to contribute large sums of money, for the purpose of making a harbour for vessels at this place, under the vague pretence of saving human life ... without being able to show that their plans would have that effect: assuming it, however, they had the hardihood to solicit from Parliament an impost on all vessels passing within a certain distance of the Land's End and the Lizard. Several tens of thousands of pounds have been expended on this senseless undertaking, which has utterly failed of its object, and made the small harbour less commodious for boats than it was before."

Nevertheless, in 1850 the port had forty-six registered fishing craft giving direct employment to two hundred and seventy-four fishermen and packers. Yet it was not a paying proposition, and in 1855 the company was taken over by Messrs. Harvey & Co., of Hayle, who carried out many improvements, which included the construction of a breakwater and lock gates, by which means the tidal harbour was transformed into a closed dock enabling ships to remain afloat at all states of the tide. But some ten years later the mining slump began, and the promising future for the port anticipated by the new owners never came. It remained essentially a fishing port.

A little trade in various commodities was carried on until after the First World War, when at last even the small china clay consignments from a nearby deposit came to an end, for the reason that Porthleven was "very difficult for shipping, which would not go there". Indeed, it had never gone there, despite the efforts and optimism of the successive owning companies.

The modern diesel coaster can get in and out of the harbour much more easily than the old sailing vessels could, but only very occasional cargoes are brought in. A small number of fishing vessels still use the port.

ST. MICHAEL'S MOUNT—MARAZION

MARAZION owes its origin to the priory of Benedictine monks that had been founded on St. Michael's Mount by Edward the Confessor. A weekly market and three fairs a year, no doubt timed to coincide with the popular pilgrimage periods, had been granted to the prior. They were held on the shore opposite the Mount, about a quarter of a mile away. The market was held on Thursdays; hence the name, Marghasiou, meaning Thursday market, corrupted to Marazion.

The priory on the Mount, that romantic islet just off the shore, was annexed soon after the Conquest to the Abbey of Mont St. Michel in Normandy. The Cornish priory sustained itself out of its large revenues from lands, tithes, oblations of the pilgrims, and bushellage levied on ships using the port; what was left was taken by the mother abbey across the Channel. The prior was under the obligation of paying homage there once a year, and rendering his tribute.

Alien religious houses, particularly if they were French, were a constant source of worry to our medieval monarchs, and the priory on the Mount was no exception. A close watch was kept on its activities. Indeed, in 1354 John Hardy, the prior, was indicted and committed to Launceston gaol for having smuggled two French agents into the realm and concealed them on one of his manors. He was also accused of sending his brother to France as an agent with secret letters and a quantity of gold and silver, contrary to the ban on the exportation of money.

Prejudice or jealousy may have influenced the case. For two years before his conviction Hardy had been at difference with the Duchy of Cornwall havener, who had questioned his right to levy bushellage on all bulk commodities carried in ships coming to the port of the Mount. The havener had probably taken the opportunity to annoy a man known to be under suspicion in matters of security.

From 1337 onwards the port was let at farm for £3 a year; this was reduced to 46/8d after the pestilence of 1349, when all economic activity was crippled.

As at other ports maritime courts sat whenever they were required, and they came within the jurisdiction of the havener of the Duchy. By tradition the court hearings had to take place at a point where the tide ebbed and flowed, and this would have been close to the high tide mark on the beach at Marazion or at the foot of the Mount. In 1455 the Franchise Court of the College of St. Mary and St. Nicholas, Cambridge, heard and adjudged a plea in which the defendants were three merchants of Brittany, against whom judgement was given in favour of the plaintiff, a St. Ives merchant.

This was the type of case normally coming within the competence of a maritime court. In 1414, on the eve of the invasion of France, the priory of the Mount was seized as an alien house under the provisions of a statute of Richard II's reign, and was made over to the College of St. Mary and St. Nicholas. It would seem that with the transfer of the priory the franchise to administer the law maritime at the Mount passed out of the hands of the havener. This, however, is only conjecture.

In 1425 attempts were made to build a stone causeway for the purpose of ensuring greater safety to ships. To raise funds for this work Bishop Lacy in that year issued a letter testimonial granting forty days' indulgence to all persons in his diocese who might contribute to the building of the causeway. Probably a pier rather than a causeway is meant since the causeway linking Marazion with the Mount at low tide could offer no safety to ships. But nothing was done, and two years later William Morton, chaplain of the Mount (there had been no prior since the suppression of the alien house in 1414) petitioned the Council for the grant of facilities to erect a stone jetty. He was granted quayage for seven years to help defray the cost. The due was to be levied under the supervision of four Marazion merchants and of fishermen of the Mount.

Subsequently the military governors of the Mount were held responsible for the good repair and maintenance of the pier and quays that William Morton had first erected there.

During the civil war the defences and garrison of the Mount were strengthened to keep it out of the hands of the Parliament-arians. The loyal Sir Francis Basset, whose family had been granted the Mount after the Arundell rebellion of 1549, was appointed captain. The cost of the defences and garrison was met with funds out of the estates of the Ceelys of St. Ives, who were thus punished for having supported the cause of the Parliamentarians.

The Mount eventually passed to the St. Aubyn family, and in 1727 they extended the quays and docking facilities, and leased the port to a George Blewett. An energetic merchant, Blewett competed successfully with the rival ports of St. Ives, Hayle and Penzance, and took away some of their trade.

Cured fish, copper ore and refined tin were all through the eighteenth and nineteenth centuries the staple exports of the port of the Mount. Imports were salt for fish-curing, timber, corn, flour, coal and iron. This last commodity was in demand by the foundries of the district, notably those at Hayle.

In fair weather many ships preferred to run aground on the beach at Marazion to discharge and load their cargoes, but in unfavourable conditions they had no option but to use the artificial harbour at the Mount. The merchandise was then carried across the causeway at low tide by pack animal.

To-day the ancient harbour of the Mount is no longer a port.

PENZANCE

PENZANCE was one of the early Mounts Bay fishery centres. It was first granted an annual fair and a weekly market on Wednesdays in 1332. This market dovetailed with the neighbouring markets at Mousehole on Tuesdays and at Marazion on Thursdays, allowing fish merchants and fishermen to attend each in turn. A manorial fishing hamlet, Penzance was let at farm by the Duchy of Cornwall havener for 12/- a year.

As Mousehole, only two miles to the south-west, declined, so Penzance grew. There was a gradual movement of population into Penzance from the densely populated district to the west and south-west, making it early in the fifteenth century the heart of the West Penwith region.

In 1404 Thomas Lord Berkeley acquired by right of marriage the manor of Alverton, on which Penzance stood. A national figure, and supporter of the Lancastrian usurper, he was a member of the delegation sent by Parliament to notify Richard II of his deposition. He was appointed Admiral of the South and West in 1403 in a critical period of our maritime history. In 1404 when the more westerly parts of the Channel and the Bay of Biscay were infested with hostile French vessels, he was given command of a large convoy going to Bordeaux. On his return he was sent to cut off from its fleet the French force that had been landed in South Wales to march on Worcester. He destroyed or captured twenty-eight enemy ships, ending all hopes of French victory. Later, in the absence of Henry V on his Agincourt expedition, Berkeley was appointed a member of the Council of the Duke of Bedford, Custodian of the realm. In this stirring period of our history his deeds must have re-echoed loudly in west Cornwall.

In the fifteenth century Penzance forged ahead. The port was engaged in the coastwise trade to Southampton, shipping hides, pilchard oil and a variety of cured fish, much of it for transshipment in the large Italian or Spanish vessels to the Mediterranean. Penzance sent woollen cloth to Gascony. The manufacture of woollens was a thriving industry in the extreme west of the county, but if the quality was poor it was good enough to find a market in the country districts of south-west France. Penzance ships were hired out in the wine trade, and we find them arriving in convoys at Hull from Bordeaux. In 1451 the port furnished three large vessels for the naval force carrying troops to Gascony in one of the last efforts to maintain British sovereignty there.

Towards the end of the fifteenth century there grew up a relatively important general trade with Ireland, with frequent arrivals of small vessels from ports such as Kinsale, Youghal, Dungarvon and Cork.

To provide better protection for its fishing and trading vessels the community of Penzance in 1512 obtained a grant of anchorage, keelage and bushellage, conditional upon the beneficiaries using the dues to keep the quay and "bulwarks" in good repair.

Borough status came at last in 1614 with a charter that was long overdue. The corporation, empowered to hold lands and other property, at once acquired from the lord of Alverton, who was then a Truro merchant, some land which is now at the centre of the town, the markets and fairs, and the "bulwarks" or pier with all the rights: all this for £34 down and a perpetual rent of 20/- a year. It was a profitable deal. The town began to expand rapidly.

With the continuing movement westwards of tin mining Penzance had unavoidably at last to become a main tin market and coinage town. After 1663 all tin produced westwards of the Camborne district had to be assayed and coined at Penzance. More and more ships came in for tin, bringing with them a great amount of general trade. The Penzance port books make instructive reading: a few typical cargoes are given for the year 1696/7.

The *Elizabeth*, galley, of Penzance, from San Sebastian with fishery salt, iron, coopers' hoops, Spanish wine, rosin, chartnutts(?) and 342 oars.

The *Prince ffrederick* of and from Christiansand with cant spars and small spars (timber).

The *St. ffrancis* from Vianna, Portugal, with port wine.

The *Brakey* of London, carrying 16 guns and 32 men, from Alicante with raisins, olive oil and wine.

Licensed privateers with a prize, the *John* of Granville, with salt.

The *Margaret* of and from Looe with peas, glass bottles, mats, port wine, mallosses(?), drugs, pilchard oil, pickled pilchards and dry ling.(Some of this cargo was probably for re-shipment elsewhere).

Cargoes of timber from the Baltic, of charcoal from Southampton and of coal from South Wales were coming in all the time.

And a few outward cargoes:

The *St. Anthony* of Bilbao, to Bilbao with cured fish.

The *Aylmer* of London, to Leghorn with 211 casks of herrings and pilchards, and 633 "barrells ffrees".

The *Postillion* of Cowes, to Bilbao with tin.

The *Hampstead* of London, to Cadiz with pilchards and herrings.

A Dutch vessel of Middelburg to Naples with pilchards, herrings and tin.

Penzance was like all other Cornish ports in that the greater part of its trade was of an international character. And like them, although remote from the rest of England, it was far from being cut off from the outside world, as it is to-day in our modern age. It had too some coastwise trade in tin, which it sent regularly to Plymouth and Liverpool.

In 1730 the borough purchased for £487 10s. the advowsons of the parish churches of Penzance, Madron and Morvah, which it sold in 1744 for £800. This money, plus £124 2s. 11d., was expended on rebuilding the ancient pier. Further improvements were made towards the end of the century, whilst in 1812 the fear of competition from the new port of Porthleven across Mounts Bay prompted the corporation to lengthen the pier to about 600 feet, securing safe accommodation for more ships. The northern pier was not erected until 1845, whilst something like £100,000 were spent in the 1880s in finally transforming the artificial harbour works into what they still were in 1956.

The nineteenth century was a long period of consolidation, and nearly half of Cornwall's tin was shipped from the port. The principal markets for it were Turkey, Italy, France, Holland, Russia and Denmark, although nearly every other European country also imported the metal from Cornwall.

Imports too were higher than ever before, whilst the town's merchants had sufficient coastwise trade to justify the establishment of regular cargo lines to and from London and Bristol with five ships.

Early in the nineteenth century a dozen countries had vice-consular representation at Penzance, reflecting in some degree the variety of its trade and shipping activities: Turkey, Portugal, Spain, France, Holland, Oldenburg, Prussia, Mecklenburg, Hannover, Denmark, Norway and Sweden.

For long decades a regular sight was the coming and going of long trains of mules and pack horses, often eighty to ninety in number. The animals brought copper ore from the mines of St. Just, which were close to the coast north of Land's End, and dumped their burdens in a yard close to the quays. The animals would then be loaded up with coal taken from another dump, and make their way through the streets on their way back to the mines. It was customary in Penzance to store blocks of refined tin, each about 300 lb. in weight, in the streets, pending shipment. At times hundreds of these blocks would lie unattended, their weight rendering them secure from pilferers.

In 1822 there were twenty-seven registered shipowners at Penzance, and many groups of adventurers held shares in small sailing vessels. A large number of schooners, luggers and ketches were launched at or close to the town between 1850 and 1890.

Penzance has been a lifeboat station since 1803; the boat is now kept at Penlee, close to Mousehole. Up to the end of 1955 three hundred and twenty-four lives had been saved in one hundred and seventy-seven rescue operations. Thirty-one gold, silver and bronze medals had been awarded for gallantry.

On 5th January, 1867, the lifeboat was launched twice, in

the morning and again in the evening, and altogether seventeen men were saved from three ships seen to be in distress. Only two days later, at seven o'clock on a wild evening, the boat had yet another call, a ship having been driven ashore near St. Michael's Mount in the worst seas ever known there. When, after a long pull, it reached the wrecked ship it was seen that the huge waves were breaking completely over her. With great difficulty thirteen of her crew were transferred to the lifeboat. Then the captain refused to let the lifeboatmen take him and the five remaining members of the crew off the ship until daybreak. The lifeboat's coxswain exhorted him to permit the immediate evacuation of the ship, which would soon break up, but after every means of persuasion had been tried the lifeboatmen had to give up further attempts at rescue. All six men lost their lives before dawn. In the official report on the rescue it was stated that the captain threatened to shoot any of the five men who attempted to transfer himself to the lifeboat by means of the life-saving apparatus.

Like so many Cornish ports that have had a rich past full of incident, adventure, productive labour and international trade, Penzance has come to depend on the tourists and holiday makers. There is still a little—very little—import trade in coal, cement and timber, and once in a while an unusual cargo is brought in, such as potash from East Germany or timber from Portugal for making broccoli crates.

Adding to the port's humiliation, part of the harbour area has been filled in to make a car park. This retrograde step was described in a newspaper as an ambitious scheme. The main objectors were, according to reports, the diggers of lug worms. These little beasts—the lug worms—were found in the mud of the harbour at low tide. And so we progress. For centuries it was ships, adventure and healthy waterborne commerce that mattered. Then along came railways and motor-propelled highway vehicles to sweep most of it away. And now the harbour has been sacrificed to accommodate a handful of motor cars. What will happen when the road transport problem gets serious, as it surely will?

Is it necessary to remind ourselves that a harbour is intended

Porthleven before the 1914-18 war (Melville Matthews)

St. Michael's Mount (Western Morning News)

Newlyn's fifteenth century artificial harbour   (*Western Morning News*)

Mousehole   (*Mrs. L. J. Penhaul*)

to provide accommodation for ships, not for motor cars? We allow the small ports around our coasts, which we shall surely need again in the not very distant future, to fall into decay, to be used to stave off a problem which they cannot possibly solve.

Percy Dalton   MOUNTS BAY MACKEREL DRIVER

NEWLYN

IN 1340 the name was written Niwelyn, apparently from the Old English words niwe and hlynn—the new torrent. One wonders if the little brook had been there very long when the first hamlet appeared on the site and acquired its name.

Newlyn had a share in the medieval fisheries of Mounts Bay, the fishing boat rights being worth 20/- a year from 1337 onwards. It was too close to Penzance and Mousehole to have a weekly market of its own. It is now a part of the built-up urban area of Penzance.

As at other commercial fishery places the law maritime was administered by the court under the jurisdiction of the havener. In 1340 the profits of the Newlyn court were below normal, for the reason that fishermen and seamen had deserted the traditional fishing grounds "quod naves de Ispannia tempora piscarie ibidem venerunt ad male faciendum piscatores predictos". History books tell us that armed French ships preyed on English vessels in the Channel at this early stage of the Hundred Years' War, but from the scribe's note at the foot of the parchment (now more than 600 years old) it would seem that Spanish marauders were also a nuisance. Hitherto they had not ventured so far from their home waters.

The original tiny medieval pier stands within the harbour area now enclosed by large modern piers. Bishop Lacy in 1435 offered forty days' indulgence to all the faithful who might contribute towards its cost.

The growth of Newlyn into a large fishery centre came only in the eighteenth century in the great mining and industrial epoch. The mackerel and pilchard fisheries were the most important, but in 1826 Newlyn went into the herring fishery off the Irish coast for the first time. The vessels sold their catches to merchants in the Irish Sea for disposal in the markets of the north of England.

Well before 1850 Newlyn possessed the most important drift net fleet in Cornwall. The nets could be shot in either deep or shallow water, and they were allowed to float with the current, thus crossing the shoals. The fish were caught individually, each one getting entangled in the meshes. The pilchard seining nets on the other hand had to be shot in shallow water and they often touched the bottom. The fish, which came in-shore, were caught in the mass without getting tangled in the meshes. The nets, loaded with fish, were often hauled up on to the nearest convenient beach.

In drift net fishing one man provided the boat, another a portion of the nets, and a third would hire nets owned by a "landsman". Each fisherman received a proportionate share of the catch. It was said to be the poor man's fishery, the fisherman being self-employed.

Seine fishing was in the hands of well financed companies, a development brought about by frequent bad seasons when no pilchards appeared off the coast. There was no inducement for the average fisherman to take out shares in seining enterprises; he preferred to be employed by the companies at fixed wages, with the hope of large catches, which would bring additional remuneration.

On the whole the fishermen of Newlyn were active most of the year. In January and February they fished for mackerel off South Devon, following the shoals westwards to Mounts Bay for the next couple of months. Then they moved to Irish waters for the herring season, returning in July to catch pilchards until December, or to wait for them to turn up.

Newlyn was a large supplier of fresh fish to the London market, shipping them to Portsmouth for reforwarding overland from there. After the opening of the railway from Bristol to London in 1841 the fish, after being landed, were sent straight across the neck of the peninsula to Hayle to catch the regular steamers sailing for Bristol. After a good catch every available cart and waggon was brought into use to carry the fish.

Under the provisions of Acts of Parliament of 1866 and 1873 the artificial harbour and the quays were greatly extended. Since the completion of the north or Victoria pier in 1888 there have been further improvements, and a large market and trawl fish sheds have been erected.

To-day Newlyn is the most important commercial fishery in the south-west of England. Catches are landed throughout the year, not only by the local fleet, but by East Coast trawlers and drifters, and by Belgian and French fishing vessels. The port is under the management of the Newlyn Pier and Harbour Commissioners.

FALMOUTH PACKET BRIG   Percy Dalton.

MOUSEHOLE

THE name derives from the two Old English words Mæw (with the vowel sound as in how), meaning gull; and holh, a depression or basin. Thus mæws-holh—the hollow of the gulls—an apt topographical description, still valid to-day. But in the Middle Ages thousands of squawking scavenging gulls must have frequented this great fishery centre.

The earlier Cornish name Porth Enys—the porth near the islet—began to drop out late in the thirteenth century.

Like Penzance and Newlyn, Mousehole grew up under the protection of Alverton Manor, which belonged to the Crown and was granted by King John to a German family known as Le Tyes. Waleran le Tyes held five other Cornish manors, was sometime Castellan of the royal castle of Berkhamstead and for some years was granted the Devonshire stannaries. All this as a reward for his services to the King.

Porth Enys must certainly have had a fishery back in 1202 when a group of Bayonne merchants held the curing rights and the pre-emption of certain types of fish throughout Cornwall. It was undoubtedly used as a passage port for pilgrims going to Santiago de Compostela in Spain, to Rome and to the Holy Land in the wake of the Crusaders. One route to Italy and Palestine was by way of Oléron, Bordeaux, Toulouse and Narbonne. By sailing from Mounts Bay the pilgrims were able to include the then renowned St. Michael's Mount in their itinerary. The preceptory of the Knights Templar at neighbouring Madron, on Alverton Manor, was there to provide lodging, food and rest for some of the travellers, or the more privileged ones.

Porthenesse had a market and an annual fair in 1266, possibly earlier. A weekly market at such a coastal place that was too small to be a medieval borough implies that it had an important fish trade; it was held for the convenience of fishermen, fish merchants and visiting seaborne traders.

By 1337, when the Duchy of Cornwall was created, Mousehole was the principal centre of its commercial sea fisheries. The port dues and tolls, let at farm by the havener of the Duchy for £5 a year (equal to about £350 to-day), were the highest in value of all the unenfranchised ports except St. Ives. It meant that Mousehole had a very large number of fishing vessels.

The main fisheries were hake, conger, mackerel and pilchards, and there was a large fish-curing industry. The pilchard occurs in medieval documents as "pilcher", derived from pilseir, a Celtic word for small herring.

The fishermen of medieval Mousehole enjoyed a measure of freedom denied to the peasants, who were legally tied to the manor in a condition of serfdom. Those who could not afford to buy or build a fishing boat were employed by fish merchants. These provided the boats, nets and tackle, whilst it was the custom for each fisherman to retain an agreed share of the catch as his wages. The rest went to the owner.

The fishermen could dispose of their shares of the catch in three different ways: to the peasants from the countryside, who had first option of buying fish for their own consumption; to the owner of the fishing boat, who had an option on what remained of their shares, which he could buy at a pre-arranged price; and thirdly, to fish merchants, to whom they could sell whatever remained of their shares. This practical arrangement suited peasants, fishermen and boat owners alike. The established customs for the employment of fishermen and for the disposal of their catches show that Mousehole had developed a democratic spirit in its fishing and seafaring community to a degree that was rare in the Middle Ages, at least in other spheres.

Fishing was the most important Cornish industry, and fish—mainly pilchards—were the main article of diet. Many families every year salted away a thousand or more to fall back on in the brief off-seasons and in spells of bad weather when fresh fish were scarce. In the earlier part of the fourteenth century probably not less than twelve million fish were consumed every year in Cornwall by a population hardly exceeding 40,000. In addition large quantities were cured and exported, either coastwise or abroad.

The nature of Mousehole's commerce was very limited. The chief commodity amongst imports was curing salt, which nearly all came from Guérande, in the south of Brittany. Woollen cloth, cured fish of many types, and pilchard oil, used as a fuel for lighting lamps, were exported. The merchants who sailed with their thirty or forty tons of dried fish also took Cornish woollens to sell at La Rochelle, Bordeaux, Bayonne and in northern Spain. Cured fish was a common article of diet not only amongst the peasantry of Gascony, but also in English households, religious establishments and military camps there. Very little wine was imported at Mousehole. It was Fowey, Lostwithiel, Penryn and Truro that took most of Cornwall's wine imports; this suggests that wine was not the drink of the fisherfolk.

At Mousehole, as elsewhere, maritime courts sat under the open sky, as close as possible to the ebb and flow of the tide, to hear and adjudge pleas involving seamen, seaborne merchants, and fishermen. These local maritime courts were a remote legacy of the laws and customs of the sea of the Island of Rhodes of biblical times, handed down by Imperial Rome, and then by various Mediterranean trading cities, including Amalfi, Trani, Jerusalem and Barcelona, eventually reaching England at the end of the twelfth century by way of the island of Oléron. The code of sea laws of Oléron was fundamentally the same as that used earlier by the Mediterranean mercantile cities, but evolved to suit changing conditions. It was also adopted, in whole or in part, by the other maritime cities of northern Europe. The code was uniform and international in character.

The fundamental principle of early maritime law was that every mariner, fisherman, seaborne merchant and merchant whose goods had been carried by sea, when he felt he had been done a wrong or an injustice, had the right, immediately on the arrival in port of the ship, to appeal to a tribunal or court, whose members were thoroughly versed in the unwritten customs and laws of the sea, to hear his case.

Even small ports like Mousehole had to be able at short notice to assemble a court whose jurors were all experts in this code of customs and laws, which was accepted by all the maritime communities in European countries. The jurors were always merchants, seamen and fishermen. This branch of the king's justice was the entire responsibility of the authority in control of the port. In the port boroughs it was the borough maritime court presided over by the mayor; in the ports that were not boroughs the havener of the Duchy was the responsible authority; more rarely it was the lord of the manor, as at Penryn, who had to see that justice was properly administered to members of the seafaring community. We have already seen that since the courts were not courts of records no account of their proceedings was ever made during the hearings. Their business was, however, conducted with solemn ritual and formality, and according to a pattern prescribed by custom.

Disputes over rates of freight, seamen's wages, the price of fish, the jettisoning of cargo, damage to goods by sea water, breaches of contract, bad debts, collision, the fouling of fishing nets by anchors, damage to another ship's mooring cables in port, careless piloting causing a vessel to strike submerged rocks . . . such was the kind of business that the maritime courts of places like Mousehole had to deal with. It was outside the codes of law practised in the manorial, Hundred and county assize courts.

Mousehole was probably the most exposed of all the medieval Cornish ports, lacking protection against heavy seas. In need of artificial defences it was the first port in the county to acquire a pier or breakwater, the ingenuity of man providing what nature did not. The work was under construction in 1393, but could not then be completed for lack of funds. To help cover the cost the government made a grant of quayage for five years to the bailiffs and community of the port.

With the rise of Penzance Mousehole fell into decay, but a revival came in the eighteenth century. Large quantities of mackerel were then being caught and shipped to the London market. In 1849, when the port was reaching the peak of its activity, it had about four hundred and twenty-five fishermen, and in addition there were three hundred and seventy packers, forty-five fish curers and four cooperages which made the barrels or hogsheads in which the salted pilchards were packed for export. Everyone in the village earned his living from fish.

An extension to the ancient pier was made in 1840. When the government took steps in 1861 to improve the facilities at fishing ports all around our coasts a Board of Trade Order made provision for further extensions. A new pier was therefore built, and under the order a harbour board of fifteen local commissioners was set up.

To-day Mousehole, with its fishery almost completely dead, caters for holiday makers and tourists, who go there in their thousands, finding it "quaint" and "picturesque", and its name extremely amusing, if quite meaningless.

MEVAGISSEY LUGGER   Percy Dalton

PORTHS OF THE PENWITH
PENINSULA

A PORTH was a beach or a cove situated, with very few exceptions, on the open coast rather than in deep bays and estuaries. It had to be a place where ships and boats could be beached or grounded, and it had to be accessible from the interior. If high or sheer cliffs prevented all access except by water then, in medieval times, it was never called a porth. Although porths are as much a part of the coast as cliffs and headlands the word still has to find a place in the Oxford dictionary.

In the Middle Ages most of the porths on the coast between Mousehole and St. Ives were occupied in the commercial fisheries, although only two or three of them may have been inhabited. The fishermen kept their boats above high water mark, but lived a mile or two away in the interior. Since under the feudal system nobody could enjoy any rights without paying for them the fisherman using a porth had to pay an annual custom or due on his boat. From 1337 onwards the porth dues were farmed out by the Duchy of Cornwall havener, the money going into the Duchy Exchequer at Lostwithiel.

Porgorwethan, now identifiable as Whitesand Bay or Sennen Cove, was worth 12/-. In the middle of the fifteenth century it was bracketed in the financial returns with Penbrath (Penberth Cove), lying to the south-east of the Land's End.

Porthplement, sometimes written Porthplomont, may have been the ancient name of the present Porth Ledden. Porthliguygh—the porth of seals—also unidentifiable, was let for 8/- a year. In our modern devalued currency this would be equal to about £25.

Portheras, in Morvah parish, and Porthsener (Porth Zennor), on the most romantic part of the coast, were jointly worth 6/8d. Porthwyn, now unidentifiable, occurs in the fifteenth, but not in the fourteenth, century. Further east Porthia (St.

Ives), let for £6 a year, was by far the busiest of all the Penwith porths.

As an integral part of Cornwall's commercial fisheries all these porths, after satisfying parochial needs, sent their fish to one of the Mounts Bay fish markets, according to the day of the week, for sale to fish merchants. These disposed of them fresh, or had them cured, partially for exportation.

The financial returns of the rents of these porths reveal only their unimportance and the effects of the disastrous visitations of the plagues of 1349 and 1361. The farm of Nansmorna (Lamorna Cove) had to be reduced from 12/- to 2/-, and that of Porthplement from 8/- to 2/-. After the second plague five porths rendered nothing, the reason being "pro defectu hominum et batellarum causa pestilencia".

Lamorna Cove, reputed for its fine scenery was, according to a visitor who was there in 1861, being spoiled by quarrymen who, "finding the granite of good quality, show little regard for its romantic features". At the mouth of the cove "where the visitor delighted to stroll on the small paths of the sandy beach, a crane now projects from a newly-built shipping stage...". Very soon the cove was abandoned by the granite ships, and the stone was taken by road to be shipped from Penzance instead.

Sennen Cove still has a small fishery, much reduced from the useful fleet of eighteen vessels in 1850, when eighty-four people, including packers, were employed. Once a year a large shoal of red mullet visits Sennen, and a good catch of these fish is cause for much satisfaction. The shoal might remain off shore for several days before coming in close enough to be trapped, and the greatest care has to be taken that it is not frightened away.

Sennen has been a lifeboat station since 1853, and its crews have been awarded twenty-one silver and bronze medals for outstanding service in rescues in which, altogether, one hundred and eighty-eight lives have been saved.

In 1864 a new lifeboat was presented by Mrs. Mary Ann Davis, of Bideford, to replace a smaller one. One night in October 1868 it was called out after a ship had been wrecked on the Brisons rocks. Of the eighteen crew and passengers who

took to the boats only one was saved. This sole survivor, by a
remarkable coincidence, was called George Davis, which was
also the name of the husband of Mrs. Davis, donor of the lifeboat.

In the Second World War the Sennen lifeboat was frequently
called out after ships had been torpedoed or aircraft had been
reported down in the sea.

In 1868 a company of adventurers applied to be incorporated as the St. Just Harbour and Pier Company, with a
capital of £70,000, with powers to construct an artificial harbour
and basin on a beach close to Cape Cornwall, about five miles
to the north of Land's End. Although approved by the Board
of Trade, the scheme came to nothing, for the reason that the
neighbouring mines, which would have brought shipping to the
new port, were closed down.

13th Century Troop Ships

ST. IVES

THE small St. Ives headland, still referred to as "The Island", was undoubtedly at one time a detached islet. It was ultimately joined to the coast by the accumulation of sea sand forming a causeway. St. Ives itself was first built on this causeway. The town has since spread up the slopes to the west and south.

The ancient name of Porthia persisted long into the fourteenth century even after the new name of St. Ia was in use. At the beginning of the century Lelant, which had a weekly market, was the seaport for the district, but it was a very small one. In 1327 there were only four people living at Porthia for every ten at Lelant. By 1377 the two places were about equal in population, and Lelant had ceased to be a port.

In 1331 a conditional licence was granted for the celebration of mass at the chapel of St. Ia. The mother church was at Lelant, and its successive rectors, jealous of the new and fast growing fishing village, refused to grant independence to the chapel. The fisherfolk, having the right neither of baptism nor of burial at their village, obtained in 1408 a papal mandate for the consecration of their chapel and cemetery. Yet they were still denied their rights. But they were not deterred from building their own church to replace the chapel. The cemetery was not consecrated until 1542.

The important fish markets in Mounts Bay—at Marazion, Penzance and Mousehole—did much to help the development of St. Ives by providing an outlet for its fish, whether these were cured or fresh. The fish were transported across the neck of the peninsula by pack animal. Merchants and fishermen had to pay a "transentria", sometimes called a "traventria" fee, probably a tax levied by the havener of Cornwall in return for the privilege of carrying merchandise, in this case fish, to the Mounts Bay markets. This was cheaper and easier than sending the fish by sea around the Land's End. St. Ives itself had no market, and had to dispose of its fish where there were buyers for it. There were scarcely any foreign imports or exports shipped into or out of St. Ives. This is borne out by the almost complete absence, at least in the fourteenth century, of wine prisage, maletolt (the unjust or evil toll) and cocket returns for the port.

St. Ives was farmed at a fixed annual rent of £6, the highest of all the farmed Cornish ports, reflecting the very high number of fishing boats owned there. Reduced to £3 in 1349, the rent was restored to its former level only seven years after the Black Death plague. This remarkable recovery was achieved through peasants having been drawn to the place by the prospects of work and food. Fish was the one food that could be quickly and easily provided, certainly much more quickly than grain and vegetables in a neglected countryside deprived by the plague of half of its peasants and half of its landlords.

St. Ives achieved borough status in 1487 when Lord Willoughby de Broke inherited the manor of Porthia. He built the first stone pier at the port, mainly for the protection of its fishing vessels. The borough took over from the Duchy of Cornwall the custody of the harbour and the administration of the law maritime there. Following the example of Lelant and St. Michael's Mount, the borough of St. Ives before 1536 erected a lighthouse, on the shore, as a guide to ships passing at night.

The new corporation was of course empowered to enact by-laws, and these were sometimes a means of protecting its own merchants against competition from outsiders. Take for instance a regulation adopted about the year 1580, stipulating that "no foresteman (stranger) shall lande any apples peson (green peas) or malte within 6 days of their arrival within the Key". Hardly a measure likely to encourage the importation of perishable foods.

What appears to be the earliest surviving list of St. Ives' harbour tolls dates from the year 1619. A new list was drawn up in 1626. Both these enlightening lists are quoted in full in the Appendix section. They illustrate the measures that a typical, independent, self-governing borough, responsible only to Parliament, was entitled to take, without prejudicing anyone, in order to maintain its harbour facilities in good repair for the benefit of its own townspeople and of ships coming there to trade.

The right to harbour tolls, which were part of the national system of local customs, belonged ultimately to the Exchequer. The owner of a seaport, either the lord of the manor or the borough, in collecting these tolls, was only acting as trustee for the Crown, from whom the right devolved either by prescription or by charter. And with the right to collect the tolls went the obligation and duty to keep the pier and quays in a good state of repair.

At St. Ives the tolls were usually farmed out to one, sometimes two, quay wardens for an agreed annual sum. From 1577 to 1766 it rose slowly but steadily from 20/- to £47 7s. By this time the harbour could no longer comfortably accommodate all the shipping attracted to the port by the growth of tin and copper mining in the neighbourhood, and by the changing needs of a rising population.

With Parliamentary consent a new outer pier, designed by John Smeaton, was erected, and by 1770 it was completed and the old one removed. The bill authorising its construction also appointed the borough as well as some county magistrates as the trustees of the harbour. The tolls were renounced by the corporation for an annuity of £25 from the board of trustees.

The Act brought to an end the old system of farming out the tolls, and under its provisions the trustees were authorised to levy certain dues until the cost of the new pier was paid off. A reserve fund was established from which to pay the annuity to the corporation and keep the harbour works in good repair. The requisite amount was reached in 1836. In the preceding year the port had yielded £1,800 in tolls, compared with only £300 about thirty years previously.

Repeated efforts were made in the nineteenth century to get St. Ives officially recognised as a port of refuge. It felt it had a good case to put up, for thousands of sailing ships rounded the Land's End every year in each direction, negotiating between there and Hartland Point in North Devon a stretch of coast poor in sheltered bays, which had more shipwrecks than any other shore of similar length in the British Isles. Frequently many weather-bound ships had to shelter in St. Ives Bay, but they were exposed to great danger if the wind or gale veered to any point between north-west and north-east. Furthermore the harbour itself was tidal, and therefore could not be relied on to provide shelter in an emergency. Only very limited improvements were authorised, aiming at giving some additional protection to fishing boats. Under an Order-in-Council of 1886 the pier, quays and all other harbour works reverted from the trustees back to the corporation, which was allowed to borrow money at a low rate of interest to carry out the improvements.

From the fifteenth century onwards St. Ives maintained trading links with La Rochelle, Ireland, Wales and Bristol, and with the passing centuries its trade continued to expand both in quantity and variety. A typical small cargo was that of the tiny vessel Le Harte, of St. Ives, which in July 1593 brought in from Milford Haven 100 packs of charcoal for tin smelting, and thirty small oaks. Oak bark was decocted to obtain a liquor for steeping fishing nets to preserve them. This steeping took place after each use of the nets. These were said to have been braided in the Dungarvon mesh, although nets were not imported from there.

In the seventeenth century we find ships arriving at St. Ives from Bristol with such wares as lead shot, nails, steel and ironmongery, pewter, groceries, hemp, household goods, tobacco, drinking glasses, Irish tallow, Spanish wine, candles, brandy and herrings; and from Liverpool with salt, English linen, cheese and mugs. These last articles, made of earthenware, did not find a good sale in Cornwall, where the tinners and peasants were prejudiced against the use of drinking and other domestic vessels not made of pewter.

The port's trade reached its peak in the 1830s and 1840s, when pilchards were exported at the average rate of about twenty-two millions a year, the greater part direct to Venice, Leghorn, Naples and Civitavecchia. Large quantities of mackerel and herring were sent away by a tri-weekly steamer service to Bristol for the Bristol, Bath and London markets. Much tin was also shipped coastwise and abroad.

Through the greater part of the nineteenth century St. Ives

Sennen Cove, England's most westerly fishing village   (*Western Morning News*)

Portreath   (*Western Morning News*)

Newquay in the days of sail

Boscastle

imported fruit from Spain and Greece; hides from South America; brandy, sailcloth and general wares from France; barrel staves from the Baltic; grain, flour, hemp, wool and groceries from various places. The greater part of the port's trade was conducted with foreign countries.

Back in the Tudor period and subsequently St. Ives was a well-known port for travellers going to and coming from Ireland. No official records of this traffic exist, but the mayoral accounts are liberally sprinkled with items of expenditure for the food, accommodation and comfort of travellers, many of whom were apparently penniless. Wanderers from London, Germany or Holland would find their way to St. Ives, knowing that they could get to Ireland from there.

In 1488 the governance of the St. Ives fisheries passed to the borough, but it is only since 1623 that records have been preserved of some of the by-laws that were amended or adapted to meet changing circumstances and conditions. These by-laws had as their purpose the maintenance of orderly fishing and equality of opportunity for all crews. The days and times of seine and drift net fishing, the manner of shooting the nets, the berthing or mooring of boats when fishing, the system of employing seine fishermen, the routes for vessels to follow when returning to port from a stem, the length of warp permitted, the number of blowers on shore—it was all regulated. Infringements of the ordinances incurred fines. Many of the by-laws that were incorporated into the written constitution of the fisheries had long been accepted as ancient unwritten custom at the port.

In 1776, in the light of rapidly evolving conditions an Act of Parliament controlling the port's fisheries was obtained. It was repealed and replaced by another Act in 1841. These Acts were based on the St. Ives fishery customs alone, which were peculiar to no other port.

A very large amount of local capital was invested in the fisheries which, in 1850, employed five hundred and fifteen people including packers and coopers. In 1905, when the port's trade was in decline but when it was still the main centre of the herring fishery, there were some two hundred fishing vessels registered there. Comparatively few people were occupied with the financing and management of trading schooners, and although St. Ives contributed its small quota to the great output in Cornwall of wooden cargo ships, its shipbuilding resources were concentrated on building and keeping in repair its own vast fleet of fishing vessels.

There was, however, one shipowner, Edward Hain, who built up a fleet of sailing ships which traded wherever there was a market for small-cargo carriers: salt into St. Ives, pilchards out to Italy, coal from South Wales to many destinations; cargoes of timber, copper ore, grain . . . From these early beginnings the well-known Hain Steamship Company grew up. It is the only large shipping company that had its origins in a Cornish port.

Privateering and smuggling added to the excitements of the busy little port, which took part with enthusiasm in both these very profitable exertions. Many prominent townsmen in times of war licensed and fitted out privateers to hunt down enemy vessels. The prizes and their cargoes were sold cheaply to the townspeople. Smuggling was most prevalent from about 1750 to 1850, when for reasons that have probably not been investigated those taking part in it began to respect the law.

A very few extracts from the diary of an inhabitant, Capt. John Tregarthen, give us an impression of the varied life of the port in the 1820s and 1830s. They reflect the type of activities that went on at that period in small ports all around our coasts.

"The pilot boat *Caesar* brought into the Roads a ketch laden with fruit, from Messina bound to St. Petersburg." (This was probably a vessel in distress.)

"The sailors at Hayle dismantled Capt. Sergeant's vessel for trading in copper ore at 4/- per ton, on which account the people of Hayle called out the German cavalry."

"Drift boats land large catches of herrings, the Frenchmen giving 3/- per 100." (French smacks came to St. Ives in large numbers to buy herrings for curing.)

"The negroes from the French brig *Perle* taken on shore by Habeas Corpus, ordered to be clothed and sent to London."

"Arrived the Dutch ship *Enterprise* from Ferrol, with Portuguese refugees on board."

"Schooner *Eldred*, 3rd vessel launched in 12 months, set afloat in good style; some hundreds assembled on the beach."

"The Brazilian ship, with Spanish refugees on board, sailed for Brest."

"The Preventive boat at St. Agnes took a small cutter with 120 kegs of spirits."

"A smuggler with 99 tubs of spirits and a crew of 6 men, captured by the Preventive boat of St. Ives."

"Capt. Moses Martin of the Preventive Service, with the assistance of the pilot gigs and their crews, took a smuggler with 339 tubs of spirits and a crew of 8."

"The Norwegians rowed the St. Ives men in 6-oared gigs for £10 to Hayle Bar and back, winning easily."

"The French brig *Général Foix* of Havre de Grace, brought in by the *Caesar*. 4 men washed overboard by heavy seas . . . all sails carried away. Vessel the most valuable prize ever brought in. Sugar, coffee, rum."

No inhabitant of St. Ives can to-day write a diary anything like that of Capt. Tregarthen. Exciting and adventurous port life in Cornwall has gone for ever. St. Ives had its regular international trade, maintaining close relations with many foreign as well as home ports. To-day this remote place is really isolated, its sea commerce gone, cut off from the outside world more than it has ever been in six hundred years. And this in the modern age of rapid communications!

On 14th November 1807 three sailing ships were wrecked at St. Ives in a gale, most of the seamen losing their lives. The townspeople, shocked by the disaster, tried to collect money and establish a fund for building and maintaining what they called a lifeboat. The appeal failed for lack of support from the town's merchants, many of whom imported or exported goods carried by ship. It was not until 1840 that St. Ives did become a lifeboat station. In two hundred and fifteen launches up to the end of 1955 four hundred and seventy-seven lives were saved, and thirty-one silver and bronze medals awarded to members of the crews for bravery.

On 2nd February 1873 there took place a most remarkable

series of rescues, probably unique in the history of the lifeboat service. The St. Ives boat, the *Covent Garden*, was called out to the help of three sailing ships in distress in heavy seas. She made no headway and was eventually driven back on to a nearby beach, her crew exhausted. A second crew volunteered to take the boat out, and she was launched a second time. She rescued six seamen and then had to return to port, her crew suffering from exposure and exhaustion. The *Covent Garden* was then launched again, manned by a third volunteer crew, who succeeded in saving one seaman. Once more the lifeboat was launched, this time with her fourth crew who, after rowing through extremely heavy seas, had to give up and return to port. A fifth St. Ives crew then took over the lifeboat, which was launched yet again. This crew saved six members of the crew of one of the ships, bringing the day's total up to thirteen.

In 1938 during a rescue operation in heavy weather the lifeboat capsized with the loss of five members of her crew, and in the following year there occurred one of the worst of all lifeboat disasters. In the early hours of 23rd January the boat, the *John and Sarah Eliza Stych*, was launched in a gale of exceptional violence to carry out a rescue in the open sea eleven miles away. Eighty helpers took part in this launching in the darkness of a wild winter's night.

As the boat rounded the headland she ran into the teeth of the gale, and after travelling about 1½ miles she sheered as she came down on a big sea. She capsized as the next sea struck her on the starboard bow. When she righted herself four of her crew were missing. Some of her gear that had been washed overboard was fouling the propeller, causing the engine to stall repeatedly. The anchor was dropped while the mechanic tried to get the engine working, but soon the boat was adrift and dragging her anchor. Twice more she capsized, each time righting herself but losing more members of her crew. When at last she was hurled up on the rocks only one man, William Freeman, was left on board. In the first capsize he had been washed overboard, but he had been rescued by two of his crew mates, who shortly afterwards lost their lives.

HAYLE

THE name derives from the old Cornish word "eyl", meaning estuary. It also occurs in Helford and Egloshayle, near Wadebridge. Some four miles up from the mouth of the estuary is the site at Bosence of a camp of Roman type which in the third century commanded a ford across the tiny river. Here was a rich tin mining district which probably supplied the Romans with this valuable metal.

Already in the Middle Ages the river had been reduced by silt as well as by sea sand to little more than a stream. The whole of the land-locked water was then known as the port of Lelant. The large village of this name on the left bank had a weekly market. The very little trade it possessed eventually went to the new port of St. Ives in the same parish.

It was the mining and smelting of both tin and copper that created the modern port of Hayle on the right bank of the estuary opposite Lelant. Two tin smelting houses, using coal from South Wales as fuel, were set up at Hayle between 1710 and 1720.

Early in the eighteenth century Bristol copper merchants had a far better appraisal than the Cornish of the true industrial value of copper and of the great future for it. They went to Cornwall to make a survey of the resources and supplies of the ore, and then contracted to buy large quantities over a period of several years at a fixed price. When the market price of refined copper began to rise the Cornish found themselves regretting their lack of knowledge and business acumen, and attempts were therefore made to establish a smelting industry for copper. With their long experience of tin smelting it could hardly have been difficult, and it was obviously more profitable to sell refined copper at the market price and less of the cheap crude ore at less than the market price.

One of the new smelting works was set up at Camborne, but it was soon transferred to Hayle to save the cost of transporting the coal, the fuel used in the smelting process, by pack animal from the port. The site of the smelting works at Hayle soon became known as Copperhouse. The project at first made some headway under the able management of a young man, John Edwards.

Very soon another young adventurer came to Hayle to try his luck. He was John Harvey, a smith, who set up a forge at the water's edge. It developed rapidly into a busy foundry.

Together Edwards and Harvey improved the port. The former cut a short canal in the eastern creek to enable ships to get close to the Copperhouse works, and erected a weir and flood gates at the entrance to the creek. In this way the water entrapped in the creek could be released at low tide into the main harbour channel, and by its very force carry away a little of the mud and sand from its bed. By this device the channel was gradually deepened, and larger ships than hitherto were thus able to reach the Hayle coal quays.

For his part Harvey constructed the wharves and quays that the growing port badly needed.

Hayle served mainly the mining district reaching as far as Camborne and Redruth. By about 1750 some six hundred mules and horses were often daily employed carrying coal into the interior. Copper ore and refined tin were exported, as well as some refined copper and small quantities of steatite quarried in the Lizard district. This steatite or soapstone was sent to Liverpool for the Chaffers pottery and later to the Severn for the Worcester pottery.

The refining of copper ore was not altogether successful. Three tons of coal were required for the production of one ton of refined copper. It was found to be much more economical to send the ore straight to the refineries at Neath, Swansea and Chepstow to be smelted at sites close to the coalfields than to bring the coal to Cornwall, and then send the refined copper to the Bristol and Birmingham markets. Copperhouse ceased refining the ore entirely in 1806. The establishment was converted into a foundry, which thrived until the later 1860s, when many of the mines on which it depended had to close down.

A visitor to Cornwall in 1808, after observing the complete stagnation of the fisheries at Looe and Fowey, commented on "the busy scene of commercial bustle" at Hayle, and on "the pretty considerable fleet of trading ships from Bristol and Wales". If the Napoleonic blockade had crippled the pilchard fisheries, the industrial revolution in England had created an insatiable demand for copper.

Harvey's foundry became the most important of many such works in Cornwall, and at its busiest periods it employed over one thousand people. At an early date it began to specialise in the difficult technique of casting, using a local sand for the purpose. The foundry turned out winding and ore-crushing machinery, pumps and steam engines for mines all over the world, as well as machinery for waterworks and other industrial uses. When the mining slump became serious in the 1860s Harvey & Co. turned to the building of iron ships.

In the 1830s a regular steamer service for goods and passengers was opened between Hayle and Bristol, and in 1841, when the railway from Bristol to London came into use, Hayle often served as a port for the Penzance district. Broccoli, early potatoes, fruit and large quantities of fish were carried the few miles overland for shipment by fast steamers. These left Hayle in the evening and arrived at Bristol the next morning.

The opening of the Hayle-Redruth railway in 1837 greatly eased the difficulties of transportation of coal and other supplies to the mines, and of copper ore to the port for shipment. Steam locomotives were used for hauling the waggons.

Hayle was a station of the R.N.L.I. from 1866 until 1920. The first lifeboat was donated by the University of Oxford. Built at Limehouse, it was taken to Oxford for the naming ceremony. It was drawn on its carriage through the main streets of the city and then to the towpath by the river, where the wife of the Chancellor named it *Isis*. The boat was then launched, manned by the University Eight, who had just defeated Cambridge in the annual Boat Race on the Thames. It was rowed up and down the river, and then capsized at Folly Bridge Wharf to demonstrate its self-righting properties.

The present port of Hayle does not compare with the port of some one hundred and fifty years ago, but it has a small and fairly regular trade in coal, timber, cement and scrap iron.

TOPSAIL SCHOONER   Percy Dalton

PORTREATH

PORTREATH—Cornish for "the sandy porth"—was anciently the fishing porth of the manor of Tehidy. Like Hayle, the modern port was created to meet the needs of the copper mining industry. It was the natural outlet for the Camborne-Redruth mines, more so than Hayle about eight miles to the westward, and when at last the artificial harbour was built in the latter part of the eighteenth century it proved to be a great boon for the mining district. Since everything from coal and copper ore to machinery and timber had to be carried by pack animal or cumbersome waggons the congestion both at Hayle and on the rough roads leading from it demanded a second port not far away.

The lord of the manor financed the construction of the harbour works and then leased the property to Messrs. Fox and Company, of Falmouth, who carried out extensions and improvements.

In 1809 began the laying down of the railroad to link Portreath with the mines as far as the St. Day-Gwennap district. The single-track line cost some £20,000, and in its time was one of the curiosities of Cornwall. It came into use more than twenty years before the first steam locomotives were built. A chronicler of the period wrote these words of the tramroad:

"... over which the wheels of the carriages, which are constructed on purpose, run on cast iron; which facilitates in an extraordinary manner the progress of the vehicles, and greatly lessens the force of animal exertion."

It is perhaps difficult for us to appreciate what exertions were required of horses and mules in dragging loaded waggons over stony or muddy lanes, and how much easier it was to haul small trucks smoothly over rails.

By about 1840 Portreath, a miniature port by any standard, was shipping 100,000 tons of copper ore a year, and importing vast quantities of coal. That meant about seven hundred ship-loads outwards, and just as many inwards. A permanent aspect of Portreath was the huge dump of copper ore amidst the quays awaiting shipment, and an even larger dump of coal waiting to be carried away to the mines and towns.

From 1800 to 1840 the population of the mining district served by Portreath grew from 14,000 to over 30,000. It was the most highly industrialised region in the west of England, with more active mines concentrated into these few square miles than in any other equivalent area in the world. The little make-shift port had to handle the greater part of the enormous sea-borne trade of this amazing conglomeration of metalliferous mines. The whole of the mining produce went away by sea.

Portreath had a small commercial fishery, and like all Cornish ports and coves it built sailing vessels. The shipping firm of D. W. Bain & Company operated their own fleet of eighteen schooners from the port.

An occasional coaster now calls at Portreath with coal, but there is no mining produce to carry away.

TREVAUNANCE

AMONGST the Cornish ports Trevaunance, which served Truro and the mining district of St. Agnes, was unique. Five times an artificial harbour was built or partially constructed, and five times it was destroyed and swept away by the sea.

It was John Tonkin, lord of the manor, who first attempted to make a harbour out of the cove. This was before there were any mines in the immediate neighbourhood. There is no more reliable account of the attempts made to construct the artificial harbour than that written by Thomas Tonkin, great grandson of this John, in 1710.

> "The neighbourhood of the sea, which forms a small cove under the . . . coom called Trevaunance Porth, has been an inducement to several of our family to expend great sums of money in attempting to build a Peer or Key, for the security of small Barks and vessels trading to Wales and Ireland and to carry on likewise a fishery. This was first begun by my great grandfather John Tonkin in 1632, but the same being broken down the following winter before it was quite finished, he desisted from any further attempts during his life."

John Tonkin had understood Truro's need of a secure port close at hand on the north coast. In the late Middle Ages and all through the sixteenth century, rather than travel round the Land's End, the little barks—smacks and brigs and, later, ketches, of some twenty to fifty tons burden only—discharged their cargoes of coal, timber, charcoal, cloth and so on for Truro either on the beach at Perranporth or in the Gannel River close to Newquay. But St. Agnes was better placed for Truro than these landing points. It would, however, have to be furnished with a breakwater and wharves.

In 1684 the second attempt was made by Hugh Tonkin at a small distance from the site of the first:

> "But after he had bestow'd several hundred pounds in

cutting down the cliff to make a new entrance, and buoying up great rocks to stop the old entrance to the said little cove, he was forced to desist for such was the violence of the sea, that it in a few hours destroyed what he had been several months in building."

He tried again in 1699, working to the design of Henry Winstanley, who had just completed the erection of the short-lived wooden lighthouse on the Eddystone reef off Plymouth. This work, which had the appearance of being very strong, was swept away by the severe storm of August 1705.

On the death of Hugh the estate passed to his son Thomas, the author of the notes quoted in this chapter. He had been impressed by Winstanley's harbour, which had, in its brief life, rendered excellent service while we were at war with France. He too, he tells us, "was fatally drawn in to continue the same experiment." He completed his harbour in 1710.

"The foundation being great rocks buoy'd up with cask and brought there and the the superstructure laid in hot lime, made of what they call lyas stone, brought from Aberthaw in Wales, which by experience I have found to be the best for these sort of works, it growing hard as the rock itself. And thus, after severall attempts, in vain, and at six thousand pounds cost at the least was this work brought about . . ."

Yet he admitted that it could not be regarded as finished, since a breakwater was still wanting. He lived to see all his efforts come to nothing and his fortune dissipated. His work was destroyed in 1736. A small breach made by heavy seas was not repaired, it was said, for lack of funds, and it got larger and larger until it was too late to save the harbour.

At the end of the eighteenth century, when St. Agnes was entering its great years as an active mining centre, the need of a harbour was once more felt. A company of adventurers was formed and an Act of Parliament obtained in 1793 for the construction of a new artificial harbour. The dimensions were small, but a miniature harbour was better than no harbour at all. The Act contained the usual clauses and regulations governing the mooring of ships, the disposal of ships' ballasts, the fixing of harbour tolls and the management of the harbour. All fines, penalties and forfeitures imposed by the provisions of the Act were to be paid to the Overseer of the Poor for the parish of St Agnes for the benefit of the poor, and "for no other purpose whatsoever". The normal harbour tolls were of course to be used in maintaining the pier and quays in good condition.

An eye witness, visiting Trevaunance in 1910, commented that the harbour was one of the greatest curiosities of Cornwall, constructed in "a most hazardous situation" at the foot of the cliffs, and "overhung by the crazy old wooden staging" and "apparatus" for loading vessels "from the heights".

All credit to the Tonkin family for their indomitable spirit. Their contribution to human welfare cannot be measured in terms of destroyed harbour works. It is much more valuable than that.

The commerce of Trevaunance was similar to that of other Cornish ports serving a mining district, if on a smaller scale than most. From 1873 to 1877 four merchant schooners were built there. Of these, two were ocean-going, one of them running in the England–Mediterranean–Newfoundland trade; the other, the *Trevellas*, taking occasional cargoes of china clay out of Fowey when she happened to be in Cornish waters wanting a freight. She last put to sea from Port Talbot in November, 1930, and has not been heard of since.

NEWQUAY

A STONE pier existed before the year 1439 at the place now called Newquay. It was one of four or five in which the medieval church took an interest; in 1440 Bishop Lacy of Exeter granted a forty days' indulgence to all who might contribute their labour or their coin to the repair of this small breakwater, which had got damaged.

The pier was the only one on the Cornish coast in the Middle Ages that was not erected for the purposes of trade or for the protection of fishing vessels. It was put there for the convenience of ships prevented by heavy surf from entering Porth or the Gannel River, the two trading places flanking the present Newquay a mile or so on either side. The bay was well known in medieval times as a road for shipping, that is, a sheltered area of water near the shore where ships could lie safely at anchor in bad weather. Such weatherbound vessels could thus slip in behind the pier under the cliffs to take on water and provisions.

In 1586 a member of the Roman Catholic Arundell family, landlords in the neighbourhood, recalling Bishop Lacy's good example, left some money for the building of a "new quay" to replace the badly damaged old one. A few years later, in 1602, Richard Carew, sheriff of Cornwall, writing as the county's historian and topographer, scornfully commented that the place was called New Quay because some people of the neighbourhood "had attempted to supply the defects of nature by art, in making there a quay for the road of shipping, which conceit they still retain. . . . The quay has now been many years constructed, but I apprehend it is not capable of receiving other than small vessels." As a good Protestant he could, officially, only very grudgingly acknowledge the humanitarian sentiments that had prompted a Roman Catholic to build a little harbour of refuge. As the quay had no trade, and therefore no profit, only seamen could benefit by its construction.

Early in the nineteenth century Newquay at last began to grow, and it was very soon thriving on a rapidly expanding pilchard fishery. Some forty vessels were employed in seining activities, and numerous small curing cellars were erected. There was a good export trade to the Mediterranean.

Acute competition from other fishing ports, and the limitations of the tiny harbour, very soon turned Newquay's attention away from pilchards and towards general trade. In 1838 the port was acquired by J. T. Austin, the creator of Par Harbour on the south coast. Under two Acts of Parliament he was allowed to develop the harbour and improve its facilities. His plans included the laying down of a railway across the county from Par, with an extension westwards from Newquay to an important group of iron and copper mines. The port was also well placed to handle exports of the growing china clay industry to the Severn and Mersey ports, but it was not until 1849 that a small railroad was laid down to link Newquay with a group of clayworks.

The building of wooden sailing ships, from coastal smacks to deep-sea schooners, received a tremendous impetus in Cornwall from the copper mining and china clay industries, which required a constant supply of shallow draught vessels capable of negotiating creeks, coves and small tidal harbours, to take away their bulky produce, and bring in large quantities of coal, timber and other supplies for the mines. Newquay became one of the most important of these ship building centres, and for some forty years its four shipyards were kept busy, the largest being in the Gannel River just around the corner.

Following this shipbuilding enterprise there grew up, as at Par and elsewhere, organisations for the financing and managing of the local fleet of sailing vessels. Altogether about one hundred and fifty schooners and other trading ships were owned and managed there during the brief period of greatest activity. A high proportion of Newquay's population of less than two thousand took up shares and formed companies.

The ship owning interests were large enough to create and support the Newquay Maritime Association, a maritime insurance society. We thus have yet another example of small-scale enterprise, self-sufficient and independent, covering every branch of maritime activity: the designing and building of the ships, their management, the supply of the crews, and their insurance. The enterprise, as we have seen, even extended to the laying down of railroads. The Victorian era was favourable for this kind of "vertical" development, and in the small Cornish seaport communities it was more localised and impervious to external influences than anywhere else.   It was a kind of economic life that has vanished.

The opening of the main railway line through Cornwall in 1859 started the decline of the small seaports. Newquay's sea-borne trade, already dwindling by the 1870s, lingered on until just after the First World War. The last outward cargo left the port in 1921, and a year later, in November 1922, the schooner *Hobah* brought in the last cargo to be discharged at the port—a consignment of agricultural fertiliser.

The curiously isolated stone jetty standing to-day at the centre of Newquay's little harbour was erected soon after 1870 to give better dispatch to the trading vessels using the port. The railway track emerged from a short tunnel in the cliffs straight on to a wooden bridge—long since removed—that carried it to the jetty some 100 yards away. Only small pleasure craft now use the harbour.

A stone quay on the left bank of the Gannel River was for centuries used as one of Truro's seaports. Coal, slate stone, manure, timber and other merchandise were imported and carried overland by pack animal.   The Bishops of Exeter, lords of Cargoll manor, held the rights of anchorage, keelage and bushellage in the Gannel.

A mile eastwards of Newquay small sailing vessels discharged and loaded their cargoes on the sandy beach at Porth.

Newquay was a lifeboat station from 1860 until 1945. There were seventy-two service launchings during which one hundred and fourteen lives were saved.

PADSTOW

IN December 1381 a ship called the *Julyan*, of Plymouth, put in at Padstow. On Friday 27th December, at the first hour of the first tide, a maritime court sat there, presided over by Richard Wilkyn, mayor of Padstow.

At this court Osbert Hamely, a merchant of Padstow, entered a complaint against John Alveston of Plymouth, whom he declared to be the owner of the *Julyan*, in respect of an alleged robbery of a ship and its stores and equipment, committed by him at Plymouth four years previously. In order that the case might be heard the two seneschals of the court, Thomas Harry and John Faber, ordered the bailiffs of Padstow to attach John Alveston by the next day, Saturday, according to maritime law and custom.

On the Saturday at the third hour (nine o'clock in the morning) the plaintiff Hamely appeared before the court in person, but Alveston, the defendant, did not. A bailiff, answering for him, stated that Alveston had been attached by the seizure of a ship called the *Julyan*, of Plymouth, of which one John Gofayre was master. Gofayre, present at the court, begged a day's grace, in accordance with the custom of the town and of the law maritime, in which to produce Alveston, alleged owner of the ship. Thereupon, in accordance with the custom of the port and with the assent of Hamely, Gofayre was granted a day until the Tuesday following, 31st December (Sunday not counting) in which to produce Alveston.

On Tuesday at the ninth hour (3 p.m.) both Hamely and Gofayre appeared before the court, the latter begging a further day in which to secure the presence of Alveston. With Hamely's consent and again in accordance with custom this further day was granted; and on the next day, 1st January 1382, "hora prima post nonam"—four o'clock in the afternoon—at the flow of the tide, both Hamely and the defendant Alveston came before the court. The case itself was then opened.

Hamely made a full statement of his complaint against Alveston. He related that in September 1377 his ship, the

Mary, of Padstow, of 60 tons burden, was in the port of Plymouth where the tide ebbed and flowed, that is, in tidal waters and therefore subject to the law maritime, fully equipped and provisioned, and waiting to sail to Bordeaux for the autumn vintage.

He then alleged that on 15th September Alveston, using force, entered the ship, took her away, threw out the master, and robbed Hamely, the owner, of all the goods, equipment and provisions that were on board, consisting of anchors and cables, large quantities of cheese, beer, flour, beef, salted hogs and fish, cloth, wooden vessels, linen, wool and sundry equipment. Equally important was the loss since that day of the services of the shipmaster, Hamely's servant. Hamely was now claiming from Alveston a sum equivalent to the total value of the ship and all its contents. He concluded his deposition by affirming that he was prepared to prove all that he had said should the court so order him.

Alveston then denied the charges and declared that he was not the owner of the *Julyan*, but had only a share in the vessel.

Thereupon the court ordered Hamely, in accordance with the usages and customs of Padstow, to prove there and then the truth of his allegations by the evidence of six trustworthy witnesses. These, ready and in attendance, were sworn, and then gave their evidence, which was an exact repetition of Hamely's own deposition.

The bailiffs and "other officials" of the town were then directed, with the help of merchants and seamen of the port, to assess by means of the customary maritime rules and tests the value of Alveston's share in the *Julyan*. They declared it to be only a twentieth part of the full amount that Hamely was claiming, and recommended that it should be secured to him in part payment. They further declared that Alveston was a man of substance who possessed sufficient property in Devon to enable him to pay full compensation to the plaintiff.

So much for the proceedings of the Padstow maritime court. A few points call for explanation. Firstly, we have this record of the court's business despite our knowledge that maritime courts were not courts of record. The reason is that Hamely, having failed to obtain the compensation awarded him by the court, took his case to London where it was heard before the King's Bench. This court, before it began its hearings, called for an account of the proceedings of the Padstow court. The record was therefore committed to writing after the event. The full written account of the proceedings is one of only three or four such records so far known to have been preserved. They throw much light on a branch of our medieval legal code which, but for these few accounts, would be completely unknown to us. A second point about this Padstow case is that the testimony of Hamely's witnesses would have been valueless had they not been present when, in 1377, Alveston was alleged to have stolen the ship and its contents. They had probably been members of the crew, although this was not disclosed at the hearings. Thirdly, Alveston could not have been alone in committing the robbery. He was probably the ringleader of a band of men in his pay, but they were not mentioned.

Hamely's action before the King's Bench dragged on in a series of hearings in 1382, 1383 and 1384. The defence was that Padstow was not an ancient borough, but only an "Upland" township belonging to the prior of Bodmin, who had no cognisance of pleas or other such liberties, except that of holding a manor court for his tenants under his own steward. Further, since Padstow—or Aldestowe, as it is called throughout the document—had no mayor, bailiff or other communal authority the inhabitants were not empowered to hear pleas; nor had they been deputed by the Admiral to try Admiralty cases. Therefore the plea had been heard by the Padstow court in defiance of the law, it was a violation of the hereditary rights of the King, and an injury to the throne. In conclusion, Alveston's attorney pointed out that the alleged robbery had taken place at Plymouth, which port was outside the jurisdiction of the township of Padstow.

Situated on an estuary only $2\frac{1}{2}$ miles from the open sea, Padstow could not be regarded, in the medieval sense of the word, as an "Upland" town. Then again, it was a borough by prescription, and the government writ calling for the record of the maritime court's proceedings was addressed to the mayor and burgesses. Alveston's allusion to the Admiral suggests that he was acquainted with some of the Admiral's business, and knew that he had not issued a directive to the port of Padstow.

Hamely's reply was that the right of the mayor and burgesses of Padstow to hear pleas at law was preserved and confirmed by Magna Carta; that the barons of the Cinque Ports and of all other seaports had their free and ancient customs; that Padstow was and had always been an ancient town and seaport, and that the mayor and burgesses had from time immemorial been accustomed to hear pleas of all kinds appertaining to the law maritime.

In the end no judgement was delivered, for the reason that Alveston's attorney produced letters patent declaring that the King had taken him into his protection. This meant that Alveston's property was to remain inviolate and that no lawsuits could be brought against him. The reason for the protection was that Alveston had entered the service of Sir John des Roches, Admiral of the West and Captain of Brest Castle, in Brittany. It is hardly a coincidence that on 20th January 1383, the day on which his attorney opened his defence before the King's Bench, Alveston was granted letters patent appointing him as joint searcher of the customs at the port of Plymouth. For this sinecure he could no doubt thank the admiral.

On the appointment of Thomas de Percy as Captain of Brest Castle in succession to Sir John des Roches, Alveston, in October 1385, obtained a new grant of protection. A month later the protection was withdrawn on the grounds that he had obtained it fraudulently.

As we have seen, this Padstow case and the one held at Lostwithiel in 1389, followed in each instance by hearings in London, in the King's Bench and in the Court of Admiralty respectively, led to the introduction of two statutes in 1391 and 1393 restricting and defining the franchise of the two admirals. The main function of the admirals was to maintain law and order on the seas surrounding England, and their courts could therefore deal only with cases arising from offences committed on these seas.

In its time the Padstow case was also important in that it illustrated amply the fundamental principle, inherited from Roman times, that all members of the seafaring community had the right to have their pleas heard by a tribunal or court at a convenient seaport, no matter who its lord might be.

The name Padstow derives from Patrikestowe—the place of Patrick—which came into use about the year 1325 and which gradually replaced the earlier name of Aldestowe. The Irish saint is supposed to have erected a chapel there in the fifth century. The use of Aldestowe—the old place—in the Middle Ages testifies to its antiquity even then.

Since most of medieval Cornwall's trade was conducted with the European continent Padstow never became a very busy port: it was on the wrong coast. The Tudor period brought an expansion of its commerce with Wales, Ireland and the Severn ports of Bristol, Minsterworthy and Gloucester. The growing traffic with Ireland was one reason why Padstow was appointed as a post town for that country in 1579.

The beginning of the expansion of mining in Cornwall was already reflected in Padstow's shipments of copper ore to Bristol between 1690 and 1700. Refined tin, a long established article of export, continued to be shipped. Later still, in the eighteenth century, we find antimony and lead ores amongst Padstow's exports. Cheese, wheat, barley, oats, cured fish of many types, and slate stones were regularly sent away.

Padstow imported timber for every type of use, woollen cloth, glass, salted hogs and tallow from Ireland; coal from South Wales; salt from France, and later from Liverpool; linen and canvas from Brittany; peas, malt and hardwares from the Severn estuary ports; a wide range of products from France and, in the nineteenth century, timber from Norway and Sweden, and hemp, iron and jute from Russia.

In the great period of smuggling this lucrative occupation was prevalent enough to be looked upon as legitimate business. Nevertheless Padstow was a main centre of the Customs' counter-smuggling activities, and it had a collector of customs, an inspector of the preventive water-guard, a tide-waiter (who went out to meet and board ships to prevent smuggling before they were moored), a landing-waiter and an officer of excise. They had a pretty long strip of coast to watch in addition to Padstow itself.

The port acquired its first stone pier before 1536, but little in the way of extensions was done for about three hundred years. Probably a unique installation, a capstan was erected at Stepper Point, where the estuary meets the open sea, so that by this means sailing ships could be hobbled into the river. Elsewhere on the coast similar capstans were in use, but only to haul fishing boats up on to the sands.

After 1850 Padstow became an exceptionally busy shipbuilding port, at least five yards turning out schooners and other types of wooden sailing vessel. One yard alone launched twenty-nine ships between 1858 and 1870. Like other Cornish ports, Padstow specialised also in ship-managing and deep-sea trading. Already back in 1823, long before the port reached its peak of activity, there were twenty-seven registered shipowners or shipowning groups.

With the decline in its shipbuilding and its trade towards 1900, Padstow benefited from a revival of its fisheries, and in 1912 it had, with its member ports, one hundred and fifty-one registered fishing vessels.

Padstow was a lifeboat station before 1825. Up to the end of 1955 there had been two hundred and seventy-four launches in which four hundred and sixty-one lives were saved, and twenty-four silver and two bronze medals awarded for gallantry.

Many remarkable rescues have been carried out by the crews of the Padstow lifeboats. Space allows only one to be mentioned, that of 23rd November 1944. At 3.30 in the morning the station's No. 1 lifeboat, the *Princess Mary*, was launched, and went to the assistance of a ship wrecked twenty-eight miles away at the extreme north-east point of the Cornish coast. She was the Norwegian freighter *Sjofna*, of Oslo, loaded with china clay and on her way from Fowey to Larne. Heavy seas were pounding the *Sjofna* broadside on, and her crew of nineteen had taken refuge on the bridge. The Clovelly lifeboat was already on the scene but was unable to make contact in the dark. The Padstow boat also stood off until daybreak, when she began a slow and painstaking rescue operation that took several hours to complete. It meant dropping anchor and then moving down stern first towards the wreck under the control of her engine, and having to "steam up" to meet each sea as it broke, so as to take the strain off the anchor cable. The following is an extract from the official report of the R.N.L.I.

"When the lifeboat got near enough she fired two lines from her line-throwing gun. Each fell over the steamer, but the crew were unable to get hold of them in the heavy seas breaking on board. The acting coxswain then hove up his anchor and anchored in a fresh position, from which he could drop down nearer to the steamer's bridge. The lifeboat was now so close inshore that she was bumping heavily on the bottom in the trough of the seas. The line-throwing gun again fired two lines, and this time the *Sjofna's* crew were able to seize them and make them fast. By means of these lines a breeches buoy was rigged between the steamer and the lifeboat and seven men were dragged to the lifeboat through the seas. Then the line, which had been chafed, was carried away. As the lifeboat had no more lines to fire, the acting coxswain went out through the breakers to the Clovelly lifeboat, which was standing by, and borrowed her line-throwing pistol. He did not need to use it, however, for he saw that the coastguard life-saving apparatus company had now got a line on to the steamer from the top of the cliffs and was taking off the twelve remaining members of her crew. . . ."

The *Princess Mary* got back to Padstow 12¼ hours after setting out. Being sixty feet long—the longest lifeboat on the coasts of the British Isles—she was better able to carry out the rescue than the Clovelly boat, which was only thirty-five feet long. The rescue was officially deemed to have been the bravest life-saving act of the year by lifeboatmen. It called for seamanship, skill, judgement and determination of the highest order. The Hartland Life-Saving Apparatus Company were also cited "for the best service of the year by the life-saving apparatus."

Padstow is one of the very few seaports at which two lifeboats are stationed.

WADEBRIDGE

A RECTANGULAR camp of Roman type guarded the ancient ford across the River Camel some six miles above Wadebridge, defending also one of the four districts in Cornwall whence the Romans drew their tin. Although the site has yielded Roman coins and other remains there is no evidence that Roman soldiers ever occupied it.

Before the bridge of seventeen arches was built between 1450 and 1470 ships rode up on the tide to the ancient riverine village of Egloshayle. The priors of Bodmin had a quay in the parish.

For many centuries lime-bearing sand had been carried from the estuary of the river upstream for the use of farmers in this rich agricultural region. In the eighteenth century a fleet of small barges was employed in transporting the sand to dumps on the river banks above Wadebridge. The farmers themselves collected the sand from the dumps.

In the canal-building epoch in the latter part of the eighteenth century two projects were put forward for cutting canals inland above Wadebridge, one of them to reach the river Fowey. Nothing came of either scheme.

The opening in 1834 of the seventh railway in England to use steam locomotives, from Wadebridge to Wenford, with a branch line to Bodmin, brought more trade to the port. Without this short railway of twelve miles in length the quarry at de Lank on Bodmin Moor may never have been opened. About 150,000 cubic feet of this granite went into the construction of Blackfriars Bridge, over the Thames. The blocks, many of which were from six to twenty tons in weight, were railed to Wadebridge and then shipped from its quays to London.

Another important contract was the supply of the granite for the tower of the new Eddystone Lighthouse, which was erected between 1878 and 1882. The blocks were worked and dressed on the quay at Wadebridge, and in some cases dovetailed and cemented in courses, before shipment to the contractors' workyard close to Plymouth.

Iron ore was shipped from Wadebridge, and also after 1865, china clay from the newly discovered deposits on Bodmin Moor. Imports were coal, nitrates, groceries, timber, iron rails, limestone and general hardware.

Owing to lack of water in the river between the fortnightly spring tides it regularly happened that schooners had to begin their journey from Wadebridge without the last portion of their cargo. Shipmasters knew to the last ton how much their vessels could carry at any given state of the tide without running aground on their way down to Padstow, but they were reluctant to lose any freight through short shipping a cargo. Hence there grew up the curious custom of barging the last few tons down to Padstow at the cost of the ship. And there, a couple of hours later, they would be transferred into the ship's hold and the hatches closed. It was a happy solution to a small question of principle, but hardly one that would be accepted to-day in similar circumstances.

Small tidal ports such as Wadebridge would never have handled the increased trade that was to come their way in the nineteenth century had there been no important developments in the design of small sailing ships. All progress in design had been stopped by the Tonnage Act of 1773, which instituted a system of tonnage measurement that encouraged depth at the expense of beam. Under this statute only length and beam measurements were used in calculating the cargo capacity of a vessel, and on this basis port dues were levied. Economies were thus achieved by deepening the holds without increasing either length or beam. This meant that ships were unstable when light, and drew too much water to enter shallow rivers and creeks when loaded. This slow lumbering type of vessel was greatly developed during the Napoleonic wars, as it was suitable for the convoying system and had a good cargo-carrying capacity.

A real stimulus to new design and construction came with the Merchant Shipping Act of 1854, following an optional change in the system of tonnage measurement in 1836. Under the Act evasion of port dues was no longer possible, and there ceased to be any incentive to build ships with deep holds. With the new shallow-draught sailing vessels Wadebridge and other tidal ports came into their own.

Large numbers of small sailing ships traded to Wadebridge in this new epoch, and often more than a dozen schooners could be seen crowded against its two small quays. They were nearly always familiar ships, some of them regular callers at the port, others returning perhaps once or twice a year. There were fashions in the names of these small vessels. There were the more prosaic names such as *Three Brothers, Unity, Nimrod* and *Lerrin.* And then there were these: *Bessie Jane, Maud, Lizzie, Janet and Elizabeth, Emma Jane, Amelia, Charlotte, Millicent, Louise* . . . all of them called after wives, daughters, mothers or sweethearts. The idea was romantic even if some of the names were not. And then there were vessels with truly beautiful names: *Sparkling Wave, Gypsy Maid, Driving Mist, Sea Nymph, Flying Foam, Water Lily, Gypsy Queen.* . . .

But they were all attractive ships, built by craftsmen who may never have been to school or employed a draughtsman. Take this letter, written on 3rd March, 1873 by Mr. R. Neal, a ship-builder-owner, of "Modle Cottage", Padstow, and addressed to a shipbroker at Wadebridge, asking for a cargo of china clay for his new ship:

"I have a new vessel hear about 170 tons Burdon we was thinking to lunch her next spring can you load her with clay for Runcorn by the 29th of March the spring after next."

He was referring to spring tides, not the spring season. There was obviously nothing pompous about Mr. Neal. He had merely built a ship, and was communicating the fact in a business letter in a natural uninhibited style. The ship was the *Peace*, one of many fine and beautiful schooners built at Padstow.

Now, after the Second World War, only a rare motor coaster feels its way up the shallow river on a spring tide. The first was the German m.v. *Flut* which brought in a cargo of timber in 1955. As there was no outward cargo for her she made the journey of over ninety miles to Par, just fourteen miles away, where any coaster can depend on getting a cargo of china clay at short notice.

PORT ISAAC AND PORT GAVERNE

WITH its next-door neighbours, Port Gaverne and the dead and deserted Porth Quin, Port Isaac belonged to the little group of the Hundred of Trigg fishing porths of the Middle Ages whose dues and tolls were let at farm by the Duchy havener.

Already about the year 1500 Porthissek (probably "the corn port") had a pilchard fishery and a stone pier for the protection of its fishing vessels. Until the rise of Newquay it had the largest pilchard fishery on the north coast, after St. Ives. In 1850 the little village had no less than forty-nine fishing boats with crews totalling one hundred and sixty-eight. It also had four large curing cellars. The Rev. Warner has left us a description of a typical cellar, similar in design to those in use in all the pilchard curing ports. The size of these cellars was determined by the space into which they had to be squeezed. They were always erected close to the water's edge.

"The pilchard cellars are all above ground, and of a quadrilateral form, though their sides are not generally of uniform length. About seventy feet perhaps may be allowed for their average extent. The center of this quadrangle is open to the sky. Three of its sides are covered by a double penthouse; the outer one designed to protect those who clean the fish; and the inner one to receive the fish after they are cleansed, and whilst they are under pressure for the extraction of their oil. The lofts of the pent-houses contain the seines, nets, and other tackle, when not employed in the fishery; and under the floor of the buildings are contrived vats, or receptacles for the oil which drains or is expressed from the fish. Being conveyed to these cellars on horses and in carts, the pilchards are cast in a heap in the center of the area, and then taken individually by the bulkers, who, having cleansed them, place them in strata of single layers on the floor of the inner pent-house, with a quantity of salt between each layer. The bulk, or pile, thus constructed, rises gradually to the height of four or five feet. In this situation the fish remain for thirty or forty days, during which time a considerable quantity of oil deliquesces from the mass, and runs in the receptacles below. . . . The distillation being completed, the bulks are broken up, the fish laid regularly in barrels. . . . The salt used for the purpose is brought from Liverpool; it is of a course grain, serves for two years, and is then sold for manure at 4d. per bushel."

Roofing slate from the big quarry at Delabole was shipped from Port Isaac in the mid-sixteenth century until the late nineteenth. Exports went to many west country ports, and also to France, Belgium and the Netherlands. Port Isaac had its community of shipbuilders, and much local capital was invested in schooners which traded mainly in the Irish Sea.

Port Gaverne, like Port Isaac, now a quiet holiday resort, also had a pilchard fishery back in the Tudor period. Later it shared in the exports of roofing slate. The slates were carried the five miles from the quarry to the port in waggons drawn by six oxen led by a horse. Vessels were loaded from the pile, stocked on the quayside, by a chain of men and women, who passed the slates down into the holds, where they were packed between layers of hay. The slates were exported to Barnstaple and Plymouth, and to the near Continent. Coal was regularly imported at Port Gaverne, where all ships had to be beached against a wall serving as the quay.

TINTAGEL

A T Tintagel the high cliffs rise sheer out of the sea. A castle was built, after the arrival of the Normans, at this, the strongest and most inaccessible defensive point on this part of the coast, on an enormous cliff projecting into the sea. Fearing a Spanish invasion and looking to the defences of the realm, the Council in 1583 ordered Sir Richard Grenville, sheriff of Cornwall, to make a report on the condition and defences of the already decayed castle. He wrote:

> "From the sea there are two landing places; against one of them is a wall with a gate in it, called the Iron Gate; this wall is of lengthe one hundred and twenty foote, in thickness five foote, garrated, now somewhat ruinal; which was in old time sufficiente for the defence of that place. . . .
>
> By the workes without this wall (beinge the landing place), four or five of the greatest sortes of shippes may, with most windes, ride, and lay their sides to the workes and land anie companie of men; the water being ther at the lowest ebb five fathom deep, and the ground in this bay before the rockes faire and sandy for a moringe.'

In due course Tintagel joined the numerous other places on the rugged Cornish coast to which sailing ships came for the purpose of trade. For two hundred years from about 1700 roofing slate was from time to time quarried nearby. A traveller visiting the place in 1808 observed that the slate was shipped from a little creek at the bottom of a ravine or "recess", being lowered by a crane and tackle "from the labourers above to the sailors below." There were no other means of loading vessels. A hundred years later, in 1910, another traveller wrote that a picturesque wooden staging, overhanging the cove, was used for loading and discharging such small vessels whose captains had the temerity to enter this tiny cove surrounded by high sheer cliffs.

There were not many "ports" like Tintagel on our coasts, and this one was unique even for Cornwall.

BOSCASTLE

THE port of Boscastle is no more than a deep ravine breaking into a long stretch of formidable cliffs on what was, in the long era of sailing ships, one of the most dangerous coasts in the British Isles. Anyone who might to-day suggest that Boscastle could be used by easily manageable motor coasters would probably be regarded as lacking in common sense, yet for centuries the manoeuvring of sailing vessels in and out of the ravine was a routine task. Let us see what Walter White, librarian to the Royal Society, had to say about Boscastle after his visit to the port in 1861 when it was at the height of its commercial activity:

"... on each side the space is occupied by warehouses, workshops, ship-yards, timber yards, and all the appliances of a busy trading port. ... But you will be ... astonished at the harbour: a narrow, tortuous inlet, which appears scarcely large enough for a jolly-boat, is made available for vessels of considerable tonnage. It is a marvellous instance of what may be accomplished by the right sort of enterprise. A small pier projects from one side at a right angle nearly all across the inlet; a few yards nearer the entrance a breakwater projects from the opposite side, to check the rush of the waves, which set in with tremendous fury. Notwithstanding these barriers, hawsers as thick as your leg are needed to regulate the advance of a vessel. ... We have heard a good deal of late about a remarkable harbour in the Crimea; but Boscastle is a miracle compared with Balaklava."

As a trading harbour Boscastle has long since ceased to live. The port belonged to the group of small fishing places between Padstow and the Devonshire border that were farmed out by the Duchy of Cornwall havener from 1337 onwards for 20/- a year, and described in his financial returns as the Hundred of Trigg ports.

In 1536 there was still no pier at Boscastle, but by 1547 one had been erected. The Chantries Act Commissioners in that year recommended that a portion of the local stipendiary priest's wages be allotted "towardes the mayntenaunce of the said keye whyche shal be a gracous and mercyfull deede of charitie." In 1549 the church of St. Thomas at Launceston made a contribution towards repairs to the quay. But the structure was not a very substantial one, and it was soon in a ruinous condition. In 1584, at the request of Sir Richard Grenville, sheriff of Cornwall, the townsmen of Boscastle prepared for him a memorandum on the new pier that was being built. It stated that:

> "The Peire and Key of Botreaux Castell hath bene of late
> tyme twise builded, ye wch hath cost the poore Inhabiters
> and their well willers above 200^{li} & the same lately de-
> caieed, to the great hinderaunce & vtter vndoinge of a
> multitude wch thereby are daily relieved and susteyned.
> But the same key is now begonne and sett in a newe place
> by the good ayde and directions of the right worship^{ll}
> Sr Richard Greynvile, Knight, and is thought of the
> skilfull workemen and others, by Goddes grace, most like
> for ever to contynewe."

The memorandum then set out full details of the wages paid during the first four months of the work, and notes on the progress so far made. A copy was sent by Sir Richard to the Council so that the experience gained in erecting the Boscastle pier, and the "hole manner of ye workemanshippe" could be taken into account in the planning of "the woorke at Dover", and of another important one elsewhere. Artificial harbour works were not erected every day, and the small pier at Bos-castle being, for its epoch, of average size, was the newest model that could be copied. Grenville's pier is still standing, the dimensions corresponding exactly with those given in his letter accompanying the memorandum.

Since the community of Boscastle had in the first instance raised the money for building their own pier, and had con-tributed a portion of their labour free of cost, it was public property. However, the harbour, including the pier and quays, was an integral part of the manor, and always changed hands with it, the lord of the manor acting as trustee of the Exchequer for all the harbour dues and tolls. Upon him devolved the responsibility of using these monies to keep the harbour works in a state of good repair. In 1740 Mr. Cotton Amy restored Grenville's pier at great expense, and was allowed, in partial payment, to levy an additional due on all ships entering the port.

As the area served by Boscastle was large, sparsely populated and virtually without industries, other than agriculture, its trade was limited in variety as well as in quantity. The principal exports were corn, roofing slate and bark for leather tanning; after 1815 for about twenty-five years manganese ore from the mines near Launceston was shipped, and after 1865 china clay from Bodmin Moor. Imports were general hardware, pottery, groceries, coal, manure and limestone. Throughout its long career Boscastle was one of Launceston's outlets to the sea, and in the busiest periods of the nineteenth century there was often a daily traffic of horse-drawn waggons and pack animals over the rough and difficult road between the two places.

Boscastle had its own little fleet of smacks, ketches and small wooden schooners which, for the most part, traded to Bristol, Gloucester and South Wales. The port had a coastguard station equipped with a Board of Trade Life Saving Apparatus, and like every other seaport on our coasts, had a branch of the Shipwrecked Fishermen and Mariners Royal Benevolent Society. These organisations called for a great deal of volunteer work, which was always forthcoming in the small seaport communities.

BUDE

BUDE did not trade in fish, and it had no metalliferous mines, slate quarries or clay works in its hinterland. It was totally unlike any other port in Cornwall, and only existed because it happened to find itself at the only break in a twenty-miles stretch of formidable cliffs.

Serving an agricultural and therefore largely self-sufficient region, Bude was never likely to be of any consequence even in a county whose coastline was liberally dotted with small ports. The industrial revolution in Cornwall greatly stimulated agriculture, and in the district behind Bude there was a greater demand than ever for lime-bearing sea sand for fertilising the land. This sand had been used for centuries, but now the transportation inland of infinitely larger quantities was a big problem.

The obvious answer in that canal-building era was a canal. It was first seriously talked about in 1770, and although five different plans had been prepared, and had been submitted to John Smeaton for examination, no canal was cut until after the Act of Parliament of 1819. Two canals were approved. One was to be taken as far as the river Tamar at a point close to Launceston; the other was to penetrate the Devon countryside beyond Holsworthy. This one reached Blagdon Moor Wharf, a quiet rural spot. This curiously incongruous place name still appears on the Ordnance Survey map of the region, although the canal and wharf went out of use over seventy years ago.

Inclined planes instead of locks linked the sections of the canal at different levels. These planes were steep tracks several hundred feet in length and furnished with iron rails that dipped into the sections of the canal at either end. The canal barges, fitted with small wheels, ran up and down these inclined planes, hauled or lowered by means of a chain. The chain was set in motion by the movement of huge water containers up and down wells some 220 feet deep. Each container was automatically emptied as it reached the bottom of the well, the other at the same moment being filled as it reached the top.

Bude was one of the last strongholds in Cornwall of the small sailing ships. They brought in such things as household furniture, earthenware, domestic utensils, ironware, building materials, coal, timber and the like long after most other districts in the county were getting the greater part of them by railway. Until the opening of two railway lines late in the nineteenth century both Launceston and Holsworthy, centres of very rich agricultural districts, imported much of their merchandise through Bude and its canals. These were finally closed in 1884.

Several small sailing ships were launched at Bude, which also had extensive shipowning interests. The little port, remote from towns of any size, had its shipping agents, brokers, shipowners, merchants and banks busily engaged in seaborne trade. All this activity has completely gone, and Bude is just a ghost of its former self.

The sections of maps appearing on pages 147-9 were reproduced from the following originals:

Page 147 Ordnance Survey One Inch Sheet No. 347, Bodmin, published in 1896.

Page 148 Ordnance Survey One Inch Sheet No. 352, Falmouth, published in 1890.

Page 149 Ordnance Survey One Inch Sheet No. 351, Penzance, published in 1888.

St IVES

R. HAYLE

The Leland or
St Ives Head
Pen Olva
Clodgy Point
Carn Crows
Burthallan
Trowan
Stennack
Hellesveor
St Ives Consols Mine
Corva
Penbeagle
Tregenna Castle
Carrack Gladden
Black Cliff
Wheal I
United Mine
Carn Stabba
Trevega
Trelyon
Chy-an-gweal
Porth Kidney Sands
Phill
Rosewall Hill
Lower Busow
Halse Town
Vorvas
Carninney
Longstone
Stone Cross
Chlodnr
Towednack
Higher Busow
Baldoon
Vorvas Crease
Trewartha
Stone Cross
Cold Harbour
Nance
Mount Douglas
Laity
Trenoweth
Uny Lelant
Amalveor
Penderleath
Trink Hill
Trink
Trevarrack
Georgia
Amalwhidden
Bolenna
Cripple's Ease
Brunnion
Trevethoe
Mennor
China Clay Works
Amalebrea
Nancledra
Ninnesbridge
Trevcron Castle Hill
Trevea Croft Wood
Lelant Down
Barvis
Boswase
Tregenna
Cattisose
Canan's Town
St Erth
Castle-an-Dinas
Higher Trenowin
Ashtown Mill
Cucurrian
Collurian
Pelgrean
Whitecross
Rosevidney
Inch's Castle
Trenowin
Nancledden
Boskennal
Tregellast
Cockwells
Devorron
Manor House
Hellangove
Treassowe
Vellanoweth
Lower Quarter
Croft Hooper
Park an Camps
Tregilgas
Brighton
Penberthy
Higher Tremenheere
Tregassack
Lower Tremenheere
Ludgvan
Crowlas
Rospeath
Trenhall
Trevarthian
Penberthy Cross
Kenegie
Ludgvan House
Bowgyhere
Trevean
Gulval
Totren
Tregarthen
Trithall
Clynoweth
Tregathenan
Newtown
Bog Inn
Gwallon
Plain-an-gwarry
St Hilary
Higher Downs
Tregurtha Downs
Goldsithney
Perran Downs
Marazion or Market Jew
Cottle's Barn
St Michael's Mount
Monastery
Ednie
Perran Uthnoe
Trebiston

APPENDIX A

CESTE endenture tesmoigne que Johan Michel Sergeant darmes nostre Seigneur le Roi ad paiez et deliverez a Benet Chepman mestre de la nief appellee le Katerine de Loo portage de cync ... nk ton vint six souez et iiii deniers daprest sur le voyage qil ferra et ad promis de fere procheinement (en) la compagnie de nostre tresredoutez Seigneur le Roi devers Irland. Et ad promis le dit mestre destre ove sa dite nief convenablement reparaille a la port de Bristow la veille de la Nativite de nostre Dame proschein venant. Done a Loo le vint et treis jour en la moys Daugust lan du reigne de nostre dit tresredoutez Seigneur le Roi dyz octisme.

APPENDIX B

ST. IVES HARBOUR CUSTOMS AND DUES, 1619 *

AND it is agreed for all ships & Barcks hencfforth taking Sandes for Ballaste ther Ship or Barcke to pay wch hath a Top ijs, the barcke wch hath no Top 3d. all straungers wch laye ther hogsetts of fishe or lyme on the peere or kaye to paye for ech tonne ijd. no boats to be ther laid $w^{t}h$ owte composicion wth the key warden; All yrishmen landing hencfforth ther loades or Burden of tymber ijs ijd & ballaste of Sand to be taken at this charge if they liste to take it: And all such Bullocks as ar from owte of yreland here landed to paye for ech bullocke id & for ech hors or mare excepte it be one or 2 for private Ryding ijd: And no garbage or shels or swepage to be Emted w^{thin} the kaye uppon payne of XXs: & none without the kaye uppon payne of Xs all ballaste of Stones here to be Landed to belonge to the kaye warden.

*Extracted from *History of St. Ives, Lelant and Towednack*, by J. H. Matthews

APPENDIX C

ST. IVES HARBOUR CUSTOMS AND DUES, 1626†

For all English Barques which come with in our Peer for safgard or traffick are to paye to the Key yf without a topp 6d.

All Alients without a topp 1s.

All English men with one topp 9d.

All Alients with one topp 1s. 6d.

All English yf with two topps 1s.

All Alients for the like under 200 tonns 2s.

All shipps of greate burden above 200 tonns accordinge to Englishe accompts 2s.

All Alients for the like 4s.

All Englishe that ballast themselves with sande without a topp to pay for it 8d.

All Englishe for ballast of sande with one topp 1s. 4d.

All such as have two topps for the like 2s.

All Alients Dubble that rate.

All boats, barques and shipps that shall take in ballast of stones within our Peer must buy itt of the wardens of the Key for the yere beinge, except they fetch itt with their owne boates and companie.

All Townes men that roule ffishe on the Key or sande except for their owne accompt and ventred to sea are to paye as much as any stranger English except herring And all English for roulinge on the sande to paye for the toun jd.

All allients for roulinge on the sande to pay p toun ijd.

All Englishe on the Key ijd.

All allients iiijd.

All Herringe to paye that shalbe laden out of our peor by an Englishe man p barrell jd.

By an Allient jd.

All beere that shalbe brought from any other place and not brued here, yf landed wheather by Townes man or stranger to paye for everie Kinter Kin to the Key jd, barrel ijd, hogshead iiijd, pipe or butt viijd.

All Irishe men landinge their tymber here to paye 2s. 1d. and they may take in sande ballast ffree.

All bullocks or horses sett on shore out of Irelande to paye for everie bullocke jd.

For everie horse or Nagge ijd.

No Dead bullocke or horse to be left 24 houres on the sande in payne of three shillings ffower pence to be payd to the Key warden 3s. iiijd.

And noe garbadge of ffishe or stinkinge ffishe to be cast above full sea marke att neape tide on the sande, on payne of 3s. 4d. to be payde unto the Key wardens 3s. 4d.

No kinde of ballast of stones, hells or swepage to be landed within the Key on payne of 20s. and none without the Key head on payne of Tenn shillings.

All ballast of stones or otherwise here to be landed to be longe to the Key warden or his ffarmor.

And the bushelledge to be paide to the Key by all straungers Englishe and Alients as to the Lorde of the soyle: Townsmen only to be ffree.

All ballast of stone shall be landed by the m^r or owner of the Barke or Shipp that lande itt, above full sea Marke, or on the Key where the Key warden shall appoint, att the cost of the m^r or owner of the said shippe or Barke and not given or soulde to any butt by the Keye warden.

Thomas trevnwith portreive

George Hicks

Thomas Purefey

Jn : Payne

Keywardens for this yere followinge ⎰Mr John Payne
1626 and Anno 1627 are ⎱and John Cossen

BIBLIOGRAPHY

The under-mentioned original documents, printed official records, general reference works, local histories, directories, journals, etc. are amongst many that were consulted prior to the compilation of the essays in this book.

MANUSCRIPTS

PRESERVED AT THE PUBLIC RECORD OFFICE:

Chancery Miscellanea Rolls temp. Edward I, Edward II and Edward III: C47/2/11, C47/2/14, C47/2/16 No. 14, C47/2/27, C47/2/28, C47/2/31/4-6, C47/2/35.

Wardrobe Accounts temp. Edward II and Edward III (ships requisitioned for naval service, mariners' wages accounts, etc.): E101/373/26, E101/374/5, E101/375/8, E101/376/7, E101/17/24, E101/19/39, E101/21/36, E101/23/22, E36/203, E36/204.

Bordeaux Wine Customs Returns of the period 1301 to 1311: E101/158/2, E101/162/4, E101/162/5, E101/162/6, E101/163/1, E101/163/2, E101/163/4.

Earldom of Cornwall Ministers' Accounts temp. Edward II: E122/39/6.

Duchy of Cornwall Ministers' Accounts (Customs Returns) temp. Edward III, Richard II, Henry V and Henry VI: E112/40/19, E122/113/2, E122/113/4, E122/113/60, E122/115/10, E122/115/20, E122/216/18, E101/42/22.

Duchy of Cornwall Ministers' Accounts of the period 1339 to 1463: numerous accounts in the series SC 6 816 to 823, and Rolls Nos. 6 and 7.

Port Books in the Exchequer (K.R.) Series E190 for numerous years in the period 1563/4 to 1696/7.

Sundry Documents:

E101/531/15 of the year 1317.
E101/16/35 of the year 1325.
Subsidy Rolls E122/70/8 and E179/87/8 of the year 1327.
Coram Rege Roll KB 27/491 of the year 1393.
E122/113/3 temp. Richard II.
E122/113/10 temp. Henry V.
H.C.A. 24/27 No. 89, temp. Henry VIII.

PRESERVED AT THE BRITISH MUSEUM:

MS. 11583. *A Description of St. Austell Bay*, by Sir T. Phillips. Add. MS. 4434 art. 167, *A Plan of Par Bay*, by Lieut. Mitchel.

IN THE POSSESSION OF MR. W. K. ANDREW, ST. AUSTELL, CORNWALL:

Correspondence of Hayes Kyd, Shipbroker, Wadebridge, of the period from 1871 to 1885.

PRINTED OFFICIAL RECORDS

The Great Rolls of the Pipe temp. Henry II, Richard I and John.
The Liberate Rolls temp. Henry III.
The Calendars of Close Rolls of several reigns.

The Calendars of Patent Rolls of several reigns.
The Rolls of Scotland temp. Edward II.
The Rolls of Parliament of several reigns.
Feet of Fines, Cornwall, temp. Richard I and John.
The Calendars of Inquisitions Miscellaneous of several reigns.
Rymer's Foedera.
Parliamentary Petitions temp. Edward II and Edward III.
The Black Book of the Admiralty, 4 vols. 1871–1876, edited by Sir Travers Twiss.
Royal and other historical letters illustrative of the Reign of Henry III, Vol. I, 1216–1235, 1862, edited by W. Waddington Shirley.
Royal and Historical Letters During the Reign of Henry IV, Vol. I, 1399–1404, 1861, edited by Rev. F. C. Hingeston.
The Register of Edward the Black Prince, Parts I and II, 1930/1.
Ministers' Accounts of the Earldom of Cornwall 1296–7, 1945, edited by L. M. Midgley.
The Acts of the Privy Council of England 1546–1581, new series, 1890, edited by J. R. Dasent.
The Calendars of State Papers, Domestic Series, of various reigns.
The Calendars of State Papers, Venetian Series, temp. Henry VI.
Statutes of the Realm, temp. Richard II.
Parliamentary Papers of the years 1813/4, 1816 and 1869/70.

GENERAL WORKS OF REFERENCE

Balasque, Jules. *Etudes Historiques sur la Ville de Bayonne.* 3 vols., 1862.
Ballard, A. and Tait, J. (editors). *British Borough Charters 1216–1307,* 1923.
Buckingham, James Silk. *Autobiography,* 2 vols., 1855.
Daenell, Dr. E. *Die Blütezeit der Deutschen Hanse.* Vol. I, 1905.
Denholm-Young, N. *Richard Earl of Cornwall,* 1947.
Fréville, E. de. *Mémoire sur le Commerce Maritime de Rouen.* 2 vols., 1857.
Gras, N. S. B. *The Early English Customs System.* 1918.
Greenhill, Basil. *The Merchant Schooners.* Vol. I, 1951.
Hingeston-Randolph, F. C., editor. *Registers of the Bishops of Exeter.* 1889–94.
Hunt, Robert. *British Mining.* 1884.
Jullian, C. *Histoire de Bordeaux depuis ses Origines jusqu'en 1895.* 1895.
Kingsford, C. L. *Prejudice and Promise in Fifteenth Century England.* 1925.
Kunze, K. *Hansische Geschichtsquellen: Hanseakten aus England, 1275 bis 1412.* 1891.
Kunze, K. *Das Erste Jahrhundert der deutschen Hanse in England.* 1889.
Laughton, John Knox, editor. *The Journal of Rear-Admiral Bartholomew James.* Navy Records Society Publications, Vol. VI, 1896.
Leland, John. *Itinerary.* (Cornwall Section, published in Davies Gilbert's *Parochial History of Cornwall,* 1838).

Lewis, G. R. *The Stannaries*. 1924.

The Life-Boat or Journal of the National Shipwreck Institution, The Life-Boat or Journal of the National Life-Boat Institution, and *The Life-Boat or Journal of the Royal National Life-Boat Institution*, of various years from 1852 to 1946, together with *Supplements to the Annual Reports of the Royal National Life-Boat Institution*, 1939–46.

Longfield, A. K. *Anglo-Irish Trade in the Sixteenth Century*. 1929.

Lysons, Daniel and Samuel. *Magna Britannia*. Vol. III (Cornwall), 1814.

Malvézin, Théophile. *Histoire du Commerce de Bordeaux depuis les Origines jusqu'à nos Jours*. 4 vols., 1892–4.

Marsden, Reginald G., editor. *Select Pleas in the Court of Admiralty*. Vol. I, 1894. Selden Society Publications.

Michel, Francisque. *Histoire du Commerce et de la Navigation à Bordeaux*. 2 vols., 1867–70.

Nicolas, Sir Nicholas Harris. *Proceedings and Ordinances of the Privy Council of England*. 7 vols., 1834–7.

Nicolas, Sir Nicholas Harris. *A History of the Royal Navy*. 2 vols., 1847.

Norden, John. *A Topographical and Historical Description of Cornwall*. 1728.

Norway, Arthur H. *A History of the Post Office Packet Service*. 1895.

Phillips, J. *A General History of Inland Navigation*. 1803.

Price Edwards, G. E. and Williams, T. *The Eddystone Lighthouse*. 1882.

Schanz, Dr. Georg. *Englische Handelspolitik gegen Ende des Mittelalters*. 2 vols., 1881.

Schaube, A. *Handelsgeschichte der Romanischen Völker des Mittelmeergebietes bis zum Ende der Kreuzzüge*. 1906.

Smeaton, John. *Eddystone Lighthouse, a Narrative of the Building*. 1793.

Smeaton, John. *Reports*. 3 vols., 1812.

Smirke, Sir Edward. *The Case of Vice against Thomas*. 1843.

Snell, Laurence, S. *The Chancery Certificates for Cornwall*, 1954.

Studer, Paul, editor. *The Port Books of Southampton*. 1913.

Wood, A. C. *A History of the Levant Company*. 1935.

CORNISH HISTORIES, GENERAL AND LOCAL

Bartlett, Rev. J. *The History of the Parish of St. Blazey*. (A lecture.) 1856.

Bizley. M. H. *Friendly Retreat*. 1955.

Bond, Thos. *Topographical and Historical Sketches of the Borough of East and West Looe in the County of Cornwall*. 1823.

Browne, A. L. *Corporation Chronicles, being some account of the Ancient Corporations of East Looe and West Looe in the County of Cornwall*. 1904.

Couch, Jonathan. *History of Polperro*. 1871.

Courtney, J. S. *A Guide to Penzance and its Neighbourhood*. 1845.

Gay, Susan E. *Old Falmouth*. 1903.

Gilbert, Davies. *The Parochial History of Cornwall*. 4 vols., 1838.

Harvey, Rev. E. G. *Mullyon: Its History, Scenery and Antiquities*. 1875.

Henderson, Charles. *Essays in Cornish History.* 1935. (Edited by A. L. Rowse and M. I. Henderson.)

Henderson, Charles. *History of the Parish of Constantine.* 1937.

Henderson, Charles. *The Parish of St. Gorran.* 1938.

Hitchins, F. and Drew, S. *History of Cornwall.* 2 vols. 1824.

Keast, John. *The Story of Fowey.* 1950.

Lake, Wm. (Publisher). *The Parochial History of Cornwall.* 4 vols., 1867–72.

Maclean, Sir John. *History of the Deanery of Trigg Minor.* 3 vols., 1873–9.

Matthews, J. H. *History of St. Ives, Lelant and Towednack.* 1892.

Norway, Arthur H. *Highways and Byways in Devon and Cornwall.* 1897.

Oppenheim, M. *Maritime History.* (A Chapter in Volume I of the *Victoria History of the County of Cornwall*, edited by Wm. Page. 1906.)

Penaluna, W. *The Circle.* 1818.

Penaluna, W. *Historical Survey of the County of Cornwall.* 2 vols. 1838.

Peter, Richard and Otho Bathurst. *The Histories of Launceston and Dunheved.* 1855.

Porter, –. –. *Around and About Saltash.* 1905.

Rees, Edgar A. *Old Penzance.* 1956.

Rowse, A. L. *Tudor Cornwall.* 1941.

Taylor, Rev. T. *St. Michael's Mount.* 1932.

Thomas R. *History and Description of the Town and Harbour of Falmouth.* 1827.

TRAVEL AND GUIDE BOOKS

Collins, Wilkie. *Rambles Beyond Railways.* 1851.

Hearder's Guide to the River Tamar. 1841.

Murray's Handbook for Travellers in Devon and Cornwall. 1850.

Stockdale, F. W. L. *Excursions in the County of Cornwall.* 1824.

Warner, Rev. Richard. *A Tour Through Cornwall in the Autumn of 1808.* 1809.

White, Walter. *A Londoner's Walk to the Land's End.* 1855.

DIRECTORIES

Harrison, Harrod & Co. *Postal Directory and Gazeteer of Devon and Cornwall.* 1862.

Kelly & Co's *Post Office Directory of Devon and Cornwall.* 1873.

Kelly's *Directory of Devon and Cornwall.* 1914.

Pigot & Co's *New Commercial Directory* for 1823/4.

JOURNALS AND NEWSPAPERS

Economic History Review. Vol. IV, No. 2. 1951; Vol. IX, No. 1. 1956.

Gentleman's Magazine. 1800, 1827, 1832, 1833 and 1862.

Journal of the Royal Institution of Cornwall. No. X and 1877.

Quarterly Journal of Science. No. XIV. 1877.

Sea Breezes. May 1949.

Transactions of the Royal Geological Society of Cornwall. Vol. IV.

Western Daily Mercury, Plymouth. 28/5/1868 and 29/6/1875.

Western Morning News, Plymouth. 28/7/1885.

INDEX